A...
Ron

TITLES IN THE
GREENHAVEN PRESS COMPANION TO LITERARY
MOVEMENTS AND GENRES SERIES:

American Modernism
American Romanticism
Greek Drama
Victorian Literature

American Romanticism

Jennifer A. Hurley, *Book Editor*

David L. Bender, *Publisher*

Bruno Leone, *Executive Editor*

Bonnie Szumski, *Editorial Director*

David M. Haugen, *Managing Editor*

Greenhaven Press, Inc., San Diego, CA

Every effort has been made to trace the owners of copyrighted material. The articles in this volume may have been edited for content, length, and/or reading level. The titles have been changed to enhance the editorial purpose. Those interested in locating the original source will find the complete citation on the first page of each article.

Library of Congress Cataloging-in-Publication Data

American romanticism / Jennifer A. Hurley, book editor.
    p.   cm. — (Literary movements and genres)
    Includes bibliographical references and index.
    ISBN 0-7377-0202-8 (pbk. : alk. paper). —
    ISBN 0-7377-0203-6 (lib. bdg. : alk. paper)
    1. American literature—19th century–History and
criticism. 2. Romanticism—United States. I. Hurley,
Jennifer A., 1973– . II. Series.
PS217.R6A44   2000
810.9'145—dc21   99-30771
                                                        CIP

Cover photo: The Newark Museum/Art Resource, New York

Copyright ©2000 by Greenhaven Press, Inc.
PO Box 289009
San Diego, CA 92198-9009
Printed in the U.S.A.

Contents

Foreword   9

Introduction   11

A Historical Overview of American Romanticism   13

Chapter 1: Defining American Romanticism

1. America During the Period of Romanticism
by Rex J. Burbank and Jack B. Moore   27
The Romantic movement in American literature was
greatly influenced by changes in the political, economic,
and social climate of America during the early to mid-
nineteenth century. Among the era's major developments
were technological and industrial progress, westward
expansion, a growing anti-slavery sentiment, and an increased demand for workers' rights and women's suffrage.

2. Romantic Writers See the World as an Organic Whole *by Richard Harter Fogle*   32
The literature of American Romanticism expresses the
vision that everything in the world is alive and interrelated. The Romantic writers identified with the philosophy of organicism—the belief that life is a mysterious
process of growth and development that can only be
understood through human imagination.

3. American Romanticism Expresses a Belief in Self-Reliance *by Tremaine McDowell*   39
The American Romantic writers believed in a human-
centered universe, the integrity of the human mind, and
self-reliance. Their work expressed America's optimism,
nationalism, and pioneer spirit.

4. American Romanticism Is Humanistic
by David Bowers   44
The major literary figures of American Romanticism—
Emerson, Thoreau, Hawthorne, Melville, and Whitman—
possessed a common interest in the human predicament,
though the manner in which they expressed this interest
varied widely. By examining the nature of man in essays,
fiction, and poetry, the Romantic writers hoped to gain a
better understanding of the universe.

5. **American Romanticism Challenged the Values of America** by *Warren Staebler* 52
All of the prominent Romantic writers were vocal critics of American society and its values. This quality distinguishes the literature of American Romanticism—and American literature in general—from that of other countries.

Chapter 2: Transcendentalism

1. **Transcendentalism Was a Religious and Intellectual Movement** by *Mark Richard Barna* 60
Drawing on the theories of German philosophers, Christian beliefs, and ancient writings, Transcendentalists constructed a new system of religious and intellectual beliefs that emphasized the spiritual connection between all living things and the importance of intuitive knowledge.

2. **Transcendentalism Is a Philosophy of Optimism** by *Paul F. Boller Jr.* 68
Transcendentalists were known for their relentless optimism, faith in the goodness of mankind, and trust in societal progress. Transcendentalism's philosophy of optimism was praised by many but faced criticism on the grounds that it was insensitive to the problems of the world.

3. **The Role of Nature in Transcendentalism** by *Lawrence Buell* 75
Although the Transcendentalists were nature-lovers, they were more interested in the condition of man than in nature itself. Transcendentalists often used nature in their writings to illustrate their beliefs about beauty, genius, and truth.

Chapter 3: Nature in American Romanticism

1. **Nature and the American Consciousness** by *Joshua Johns* 79
American Romantic writers and artists challenged the traditional view of nature as an obstacle to the establishment of a civilization. In their writing and art they presented nature as a source of truth, beauty, freedom, and national pride.

2. **American Romantics View Nature as a Metaphor for the Self** by *Bernard Rosenthal* 84
Romantic writers attempted to create a private, interior world free from the constraints of society. The Romantic journey into nature represented a journey into the self.

3. **Emerson's and Thoreau's Understanding of Nature** by *Ann Woodlief* 92
American Romantic writers Ralph Waldo Emerson and

Henry David Thoreau both attempted to draw connections between nature and humanity. However, while Emerson sought to understand how nature could enhance human experience, Thoreau viewed nature as having value independent from man.

4. **Differing Perceptions of Nature in American and European Romanticism** *by Tony Tanner* 97
While American Romantic writers looked to their environment to inspire and inform their works of art, they seldom demonstrated a genuine communion with nature. European Romantics, on the other hand, experienced a reciprocal relationship with nature.

Chapter 4: The Individual in American Romanticism

1. **Thoreau: The Individual Versus the Institution** *by Michael J. Hoffman* 106
Of the American Romantic writers, Henry David Thoreau was the most vociferous critic of society. He believed that society—particularly government—violated the integrity of individuals by limiting their choices. Furthermore, he argued that it was the individual's duty to disregard the government when it acted without conscience.

2. **Whitman's Individualism** *by Newton Arvin* 113
Passages from Walt Whitman's letters and poems indicate that his individualism was tempered by a desire for comradeship, solidarity, and democracy. Whitman criticized the individualistic philosophy of capitalism on the grounds that it exploited the masses.

3. **The Isolation of the Individual in** *Moby-Dick* *by Quentin Anderson* 120
The lack of interaction among the characters of *Moby-Dick* illustrates Herman Melville's belief that the individual consciousness is isolated from the world.

4. **Emerson's Vision of the Self** *by Evan Carton* 128
Ralph Waldo Emerson believed that each individual had an original relation to the universe that could be expressed through art. He maintained that the convergence of the self and the universe brought knowledge and power.

Chapter 5: Allegory and Symbolism

1. **Poe's Motifs of Enclosure** *by Richard Wilbur* 133
One of Edgar Allan Poe's prominent themes is the conflict between the poetic soul—which he associates with imagination, beauty, and divinity—and the external world of time and reason. Poe employs motifs of enclosure to illustrate the poetic soul's efforts to escape the external world by dreaming.

2. **Hawthorne's Use of Allegory** *by Michael Davitt Bell* 143
Allegory usually refers to a fictional representation of reality that illustrates truths or generalizations about human
existence. While Nathaniel Hawthorne's fiction is com-
prised of allegorical elements—the scarlet letter, for example—it does not use these elements to convey a moral.

3. **Symbolism in *Moby-Dick* by F.O. Matthiessen** 149
In *Moby-Dick*, Herman Melville used symbols to project
man's inner struggle onto the exterior world. The meanings of Melville's symbols are not static but shift depend-
ing on context.

4. **The Symbols in Whitman's "When Lilacs Last in
the Dooryard Bloom'd"** *by Charles Feidelson Jr.* 155
Walt Whitman's famous poem "When Lilacs Last in the
Dooryard Bloom'd" is literally an elegy to Abraham Lincoln. However, on a symbolic level, the poem is a representation of the poet's process of creating the poem itself.

Chronology   161

For Further Research   165

Index   169

FOREWORD

The study of literature most often involves focusing on an individual work and uncovering its themes, stylistic conventions, and historical relevance. It is also enlightening to examine multiple works by a single author, identifying similarities and differences among texts and tracing the author's development as an artist.

While the study of individual works and authors is instructive, however, examining groups of authors who shared certain cultural or historical experiences adds a further richness to the study of literature. By focusing on literary movements and genres, readers gain a greater appreciation of influence of historical events and social circumstances on the development of particular literary forms and themes. For example, in the early twentieth century, rapid technological and industrial advances, mass urban migration, World War I, and other events contributed to the emergence of a movement known as American modernism. The dramatic social changes, and the uncertainty they created, were reflected in an increased use of free verse in poetry, the stream-of-consciousness technique in fiction, and a general sense of historical discontinuity and crisis of faith in most of the literature of the era. By focusing on these commonalities, readers attain a more comprehensive picture of the complex interplay of social, economic, political, aesthetic, and philosophical forces and ideas that create the tenor of any era. In the nineteenth-century American romanticism movement, for example, authors shared many ideas concerning the preeminence of the self-reliant individual, the infusion of nature with spiritual significance, and the potential of persons to achieve transcendence via communion with nature. However, despite their commonalities, American romantics often differed significantly in their thematic and stylistic approaches. Walt Whitman celebrated the communal nature of America's open democratic society, while Ralph Waldo

Emerson expressed the need for individuals to pursue their own fulfillment regardless of their fellow citizens. Herman Melville wrote novels in a largely naturalistic style whereas Nathaniel Hawthorne's novels were gothic and allegorical.

Another valuable reason to investigate literary movements and genres lies in their potential to clarify the process of literary evolution. By examining groups of authors, literary trends across time become evident. The reader learns, for instance, how English romanticism was transformed as it crossed the Atlantic to America. The poetry of Lord Byron, William Wordsworth, and John Keats celebrated the restorative potential of rural scenes. The American romantics, writing later in the century, shared their English counterparts' faith in nature; but American authors were more likely to present an ambiguous view of nature as a source of liberation as well as the dwelling place of personal demons. The whale in Melville's *Moby-Dick* and the forests in Hawthorne's novels and stories bear little resemblance to the benign pastoral scenes in Wordsworth's lyric poems.

Each volume in Greenhaven Press's Great Literary Movements and Genres series begins with an introductory essay that places the topic in a historical and literary context. The essays that follow are carefully chosen and edited for ease of comprehension. These essays are arranged into clearly defined chapters that are outlined in a concise annotated table of contents. Finally, a thorough chronology maps out crucial literary milestones of the movement or genre as well as significant social and historical events. Readers will benefit from the structure and coherence that these features lend to material that is often challenging. With Greenhaven's Great Literary Movements and Genres in hand, readers will be better able to comprehend and appreciate the major literary works and their impact on society.

INTRODUCTION

In 1941, literary critic F.O. Matthiessen introduced the term "American Renaissance" to refer to the literary ferment taking place in the United States between the late 1830s and the beginning of the Civil War in 1861. The period culminated in the 1850s, when some of the greatest books of all time—Herman Melville's *Moby-Dick*, Nathaniel Hawthorne's *The Scarlet Letter*, Walt Whitman's *Leaves of Grass*, and Henry David Thoreau's *Walden*—appeared on the heels of one another. While Matthiessen's term reflects the spirit of the movement, American Romanticism was not technically a renaissance, but a nascence—a birth. The American Romantics were the first to establish a literary tradition that expressed the unique character of America. They recognized the inadequacy of European modes of expression to capture the expanding, constantly shifting landscape of America—a landscape that was simultaneously wild and urban, rough-hewn and refined.

The genesis of the movement is difficult to pinpoint. However, the American Romantics were undoubtedly influenced by the dramatic political and social changes taking place in the early nineteenth century. Andrew Jackson, president from 1829–1837, posed a challenge to the aristocracy with his belief in a democratic, egalitarian society. The philosophy of manifest destiny was causing the country—which was already sprawling and heterogeneous—to expand westward at a rapid rate. A different type of growth was occurring in the North, as industrialization transformed small towns into urban centers. At the same time, conflict over slavery was creating a serious rift between the South and the North.

The Romantics had disparate reactions to the changes taking place in America. On the surface, American Romanticism's most prominent writers—Ralph Waldo Emerson, Nathaniel Hawthorne, Herman Melville, Edgar Allan Poe,

Henry David Thoreau, and Walt Whitman—appear to be more dissimilar than alike. Attempts to unify the group by applying the characteristics commonly associated with Romanticism are often fruitless. For example, if Romanticism is defined as idealism, Hawthorne and Melville, who were more pessimistic, do not fit in. Alternatively, if Romanticism is viewed as an expression of nationalism, one would have to exclude Poe, whose writing contains no details that are distinctly American. Furthermore, the writers of this period did not adhere to any one form, instead experimenting in novels (often referred to as "romances"), short stories, tales, essays, journals, poetry, and travelogues.

Although the American Romantics adopted a variety of styles and themes, they were unified by a concern with the internal world—the world of the mind. The American Romantics were less interested in how people related to each other than they were with people as individuals. In a society that was complex and inconstant, the Romantics turned inward for a source of truth, examining questions of human identity, imagination, and intuition. Some writers, such as Emerson, Thoreau, and Whitman, regarded the individual with optimism and confidence. Other Romantics, Hawthorne and Melville, for example, explored the individual's isolation from society by providing complex psychological portraits of their protagonists.

The instability of American society also inspired the Romantic faith in nature. For the American Romantics, nature was a place of beauty, simplicity, and truth. The Romantics revered nature for its own sake, but also looked to nature as a metaphor for the human experience.

Themes of individualism and nature are among the many aspects of American Romanticism examined in *American Romanticism: Great Literary Movements*, an anthology of essays written by some of the most well-known critics of American Romanticism. It is the editor's hope that this anthology will assist the reader in understanding the work that emerged during this exceptional period in the history of American literature.

A HISTORICAL OVERVIEW
OF AMERICAN ROMANTICISM

According to literary folklore, the movement known as American Romanticism can be traced back to a specific date, August 31, 1837, when Ralph Waldo Emerson addressed the Phi Beta Kappa Society at Harvard College. In his speech, called "The American Scholar," Emerson entreated the writers of America to establish their literary independence from Europe. He announced

> Perhaps the time is already come . . . when the sluggard intellect of this continent will look from under its iron lids, and fill the postponed expectation of the world with something better than the exertions of mechanical skill. Our day of dependence, our long apprenticeship to the learning of other lands, draws to a close. The millions, that around us are rushing into life, cannot always be fed on the sere remains of foreign harvests. Events, actions arise, that must be sung, that will sing themselves.[1]

These words have become known as the herald of a dazzling spell of creative energy that produced some of the most esteemed works of all time: Herman Melville's *Moby-Dick*, Nathaniel Hawthorne's *The Scarlet Letter*, Walt Whitman's *Leaves of Grass*, Henry David Thoreau's *Walden*, the essays of Emerson, and the short stories of Edgar Allan Poe. The literature of American Romanticism, written between the late 1830s and the onset of the Civil War in 1861, is considered the first illustration of American literary genius.

The previous generation of writers, who had been born immediately after the revolution—namely, Washington Irving, James Fenimore Cooper, and William Cullen Bryant—had attempted to represent the American experience, but were constrained by their adherence to European literary models. As Larzer Ziff, author of *Literary Democracy*, contends, "A good deal of what [Irving, Cooper, and Bryant] observed in their society failed to register in their writing because they had no precedent for regarding it worthy of being presented."[2] The American Romantics established that precedent. For the first time in history, the literature of America was not written to fit into the tradition of other countries; instead, it created a tradition of its own.

This is not to say that American Romanticism was not influenced by the literature of other countries. In fact, the American Romantics borrowed liberally from the forms exhibited in Europe—particularly England—during the early nineteenth century. One such form was the Gothic novel, which dominated British literature during the late 1700s and early 1800s, reaching its pinnacle in 1818 with the publication of Mary Shelley's *Frankenstein*. Drawing on images of graveyards, dark forests, and monasteries, the Gothic novel explored the supernatural and grotesque. Some of the Gothic writers, such as Mary Shelley, were also part of the Romantic movement that was beginning to flourish in England. Initially developed in Europe during the 1700s, the philosophy of Romanticism favored nature over the city, the individual over society, and emotion over rationality. Romanticism was embraced by the most famous nineteenth century British poets: William Blake, Lord Byron, William Wordsworth, John Keats, and Percy Bysshe Shelley. However, the prominent British novelists of that era, such as Jane Austen, Charles Dickens, and Anthony Trollope, employed Romantic elements in their work, but were more interested in creating realistic representations of society through the use of abundant detail.

American Romantics combined elements of Gothic literature, Romanticism, and the British novel to create a new form: the American romance. The intent of the American romance was to examine the intersection between fantasy and reality. In his introduction to *The Scarlet Letter*, titled "The Custom House," Hawthorne describes the domain of romance as "somewhere between the real world and fairyland, where the Actual and the Imaginary may meet, and each imbue itself with the nature of the other."[3]

Although the events it portrays are often realistic, a romance is intended to be read primarily on a figurative level. Melville, Hawthorne, and Poe often constructed their figurative representations through the use of allegory and symbolism. Hawthorne's narrative, "The Birth-mark," illustrates how Romantic writers employed allegory and symbolism in their fiction. Over the course of the story, the protagonist,

Aylmer, grows increasingly repulsed by a small red birth-mark on his wife Georgiana's cheek—which he feels is the only thing marring her perfect beauty. Repulsed to the point of obsession, Aylmer concocts a potion that he hopes will eliminate the birthmark. His potion does cause the birth-mark to evaporate, but it also kills Georgiana.

Viewed allegorically, Aylmer's failed attempt at removing Georgiana's birthmark—a symbol of human imperfection—represents the futility of seeking spiritual perfection in the material world. As professor Deborah L. Madsen writes, "[Aylmer attempts] to remove the single sign of his wife's earthly mortality: the birth-mark which stands as her 'visible mark of earthly imperfection.' . . . Aylmer becomes obsessed with the scientific redemption of fallen nature which he hopes to achieve by perfecting his wife's beauty. He misguidedly seeks a spiritual absolute in the form of a literal reality."[4]

ORGANIC STYLE

While American fiction writers were using allegory and symbolism to create romances, American poets of the era were attempting to draw a connection between art and nature. Influenced by British Romantic Samuel Taylor Coleridge, who asserted that a poem should aspire to the wholeness of a living thing, Emerson developed the theory of organic style. Organic style was a manifestation of organicism—the Romantic view that everything in the world is alive and interrelated. As Emerson writes, "[I]t is not metres, but a metre-making argument, that makes a poem,—a thought so passionate and alive, that, like the spirit of a plant or an animal, it has an architecture of its own, and adorns nature with a new thing."[5]

Whitman took this belief even one step further by completely discarding meter, rhyme schemes, and traditional forms. In doing so, he broke from a literary tradition that had guided poetry for centuries. No one knows exactly what prompted Whitman to invent free verse. Some speculate that he was inspired by the Bible's Psalms, while others claim that his themes of liberty, individualism, and optimism demanded a new, freer form. Regardless, Whitman's work changed the character of poetry in America and in the world. His invention of free verse is considered by many to be the single most important innovation in poetry.

THE RISE OF DEMOCRATIC THOUGHT

While American Romanticism created new styles, it is known more for its development of ideas. In general, the movement can be characterized by four main tenets: nationalistic pride, optimism, a love of nature, and a belief in the superiority of the individual. These themes were influenced in part by the political and social forces guiding the country during the early to mid-nineteenth century.

Politically, the most significant factor of the time was the rise of what was referred to as Jacksonian democracy. Although Americans typically view democracy as an integral part of the nation's history, the concept of democracy as it is known today did not appear until the first quarter of the nineteenth century. In fact, for those who controlled the country's wealth and power in the early 1800s, the word "democracy" did not connote freedom and justice, but anarchy. Therefore, when Andrew Jackson, a devoted Democrat, emerged as a presidential candidate in 1822, the aristocratic class regarded him with contempt. The general public, on the other hand, saw Jackson as an ideal leader. Literary historians Robert Penn Warren, Cleanth Brooks, and R.W.B. Lewis describe him as

> a man of common origins but master of an elegant estate and of a high manner when occasion demanded, a man of hardihood, a duelist, a connoisseur of horseflesh, a breeder of fighting cocks, a soldier with a natural air of command, unimpeachable courage, and iron endurance, the hero of the Battle of New Orleans, a politician of pungent vocabulary, ruthless logic, and ferocious partisanship.[6]

With his charisma, strength, and willingness to rebel against tradition, Jackson had great popular appeal. In the 1828 election against John Quincy Adams, Jackson won every electoral vote except for those from New England. The triumph of a "common man" such as Jackson over the blue-blooded Adams was seen as a challenge to the aristocracy and the beginning of an egalitarian society.

Although the Romantic writers were not direct supporters of Jackson—only Hawthorne was a Democrat—the Romantic movement was influenced by the rise of democratic thought. By the time Jackson was president, the Fourth of July was the most popular holiday, and the country was experiencing a wave of nationalistic pride. American Romanticism reflected the optimism of a young, expanding country whose possibilities were limitless. Of the American Romantics, Emerson and Whitman were the most patriotic; Poe, who refused to identify particular places in his work, was probably the least. Emerson suspected that America was destined to be a leading nation, not in financial terms, but in generosity of spirit. Whitman agreed. He wrote that "the chief reason for the being of the United States of America is to bring about the common good will of all mankind, the solidarity of the world."[7]

Yet at the same time that the rise of democracy was generating optimism, the country was also experiencing change and discord. The North and South quarreled over the ethics of slavery; the philosophy of "manifest destiny" was inciting aggressive expansion into the West; and northern industrialization was transforming intimate communities into bustling, anonymous cities. The American landscape was fluctuating and unpredictable. Attempting to locate a stable center amidst an increasingly complex and chaotic world, the American Romantics turned to the self. The Romantic hero of America is not a person embroiled in social conflict, but an isolated individual relying upon inner resources. As critic Kathryn VanSpanckeren writes,

> America was, in part, an undefined, constantly moving frontier populated by immigrants speaking foreign languages and following strange and crude ways of life. Thus the main character in American literature might find himself alone among cannibal tribes, as in Melville's *Typee*, or exploring a wilderness like the grave, like Poe's solitary individuals, or meeting the devil walking in the forest, like Hawthorne's Young Goodman Brown. Virtually all the great American protagonists have been "loners." The democratic individual had, as it were, to invent himself.[8]

Many of the Romantic writers regarded this solitude as a source of optimism. Emerson's essays proclaim a philosophy of self-reliance—a philosophy put into practice by Thoreau at Walden Pond. Whitman, in his poems from *Leaves of Grass*, expresses a feeling of triumphant individualism and self-love. For Poe, the internal world of dreams and imagination was superior to the external world.

Hawthorne and Melville, however, had a darker vision of the self. Hawthorne, who shunned society for much of his life, was concerned with human isolation. The supreme example of this loneliness is found in Hester Prynne, the heroine of *The Scarlet Letter*, who chooses a life of isolation even after she has been allowed to rejoin society.

Melville was not interested with isolation so much as alienation. While his characters interact with one another, they maintain a private and internal dignity that is untouched by the world around them.

THE RISE OF INDUSTRIALIZATION

One of the most significant changes taking place in nineteenth century America was the rise of industrialization, which brought telegraph lines, railroads, and factories to the nation's cities. The Romantic writers were beginning to see the negative effects of urban life: its frantic pace, lack of connectedness or conscience, and the increased value it placed on material goods. In order to escape what they perceived as a materialistic and spiritually void society, the American Romantics turned to nature, which they saw as the source of simplicity, truth, and beauty.

Thoreau was one of the most vociferous critics of industrialization. His disregard for material possessions was so great that he refused a welcome mat given to him because he could not trouble himself to shake it out, and when he realized that the three limestone paperweights on his desk required daily dusting, he promptly threw them out the window. Thoreau's desire for a simple and natural existence motivated his famous experiment at Walden Pond. In 1845, Thoreau left society and built a one-room cabin for himself in the woods near Walden Pond in Massachusetts, where he made a living by occasional day labor and selling produce that he grew on a small farm. During his two-year stay at Walden Pond, he wrote his most celebrated work: *Walden*, a book that is simultaneously considered a travelogue, a study of nature, a journal, and a philosophical treatise. *Walden* expressed the Romantic hope for a closer communion between man and nature.

TRANSCENDENTALISM

Romantic thought was also influenced by the Transcendentalist movement. Simultaneously a religion, philosophy, and mode of life, Transcendentalism constructed a new way of perceiving God, man, and the acquisition of knowledge. In practical terms, the Transcendentalists were a group of intellectuals residing in New England between the late 1830s and late '40s. In his editorial introduction to the first issue of *The Dial*, Emerson described the character of the

Transcendentalists:

> Those who share in [Transcendentalism] have no external organization, no badge, no creed, no name. They do not vote, or print, or even meet together. They do not know each other's faces or names. They are united only in a common love of truth and love of its work. They are of all conditions and constitutions. Of these acolytes, if some are happily born and well-bred, many are no doubt ill-dressed, ill-placed, ill-made, with as many scars of hereditary vice as other men. Without pomp, without trumpet, in lonely and obscure places, in solitude, in servitude, in compunctions and privations, trudging beside the team in the dusty road or drudging a hireling in other men's cornfields, schoolmasters, who teach a few children the rudiments for a pittance, ministers of small parishes of the obscurer sects, lone women in dependent condition, matrons and young maidens, rich and poor, beautiful and hard-favored, without concert or proclamation of any kind, they have silently given in their several adherence to a new hope, and in all companies do signify a greater trust in the nature and resources of man, than the laws or the popular opinions will well allow.[9]

Although the Transcendentalists defied categorization, they did have an organization of sorts. The Transcendentalist Club, as it would be called afterwards, was a discussion group that began its irregular meetings in 1836. It brought together the most prominent intellectuals of New England: Ralph Waldo Emerson, Frederic Henry Hedge, George Ripley, Theodore Parker, Henry David Thoreau, Margaret Fuller, and Bronson Alcott (father of Louisa May Alcott). A tangible product of these discussions took form in *The Dial*, a Transcendentalist magazine published during the years 1840–1844 and edited by Emerson and Fuller. *The Dial* was not only a forum for Transcendentalist thought, but it also gave voice to some of the most talented and thoughtful writers of the era. According to writer Frederick Ives Carpenter, "*The Dial* probably published more famous articles and poems by more famous men of letters than any other American magazine of its small scope and brief span."[10] Among the most significant works published in *The Dial* were Emerson's first and second set of essays, Thoreau's *Natural History of Massachusetts*, and one of the first feminist texts of America, Fuller's *Women in the Nineteenth Century*.

THE ORIGINS OF TRANSCENDENTALISM

Emerson, the Transcendentalist Club's unofficial leader, was the first to develop and articulate the principles of Transcendentalism. It is said that Emerson's philosophy is shaped by such various sources as the ancient Greeks, oriental mystics, German idealists, and contemporary Christian ministers.

Transcendentalism began as an outgrowth of Unitarianism. The first liberal religion in America, Unitarianism challenged the Calvinistic belief that man was inherently corrupt. Instead, it offered an optimistic view of mankind, encouraging its followers to rely on their individual consciences as moral guides. Transcendentalists embraced Unitarianism's faith in the individual, but were dissatisfied with the religion's emphasis on rationalism. Unitarianism was grounded in the work of eighteenth-century philosopher John Locke, who theorized that the mind was empty until it accumulated knowledge through experiences. According to critics Robert Penn Warren, Cleanth Brooks, and R.W.B. Lewis, "Locke, and [David] Hume after him, held that the mind begins as a blank page—a *tabula rasa*—and that all knowledge develops from sensations."[11]

Emerson, who was a minister in the Unitarian Church until 1832, referred to this aspect of Unitarianism as "corpse-cold." He looked to the German idealists—particularly philosopher Immanuel Kant—for an alternative view. Kant, in direct opposition to Locke, asserted that man knows things that his senses cannot tell him. Professors Rex J. Burbank and Jack B. Moore maintain that Kant's ideal world

> exists beyond the cognitive power of the senses and . . . can be reached by man's superior intuitive powers. Man has *a priori* knowledge of the world, gained not from sense impressions but from categories internal to his own mind. The power to transcend the world of sensuous particulars and to reach absolutes of time and space and truth emanates from some ultimate source beyond man, but man contains this power to some extent, just as a room might retain a bit of light from some greater flame.[12]

This view formed the basis for one of Emerson's most celebrated concepts—the belief that every person belongs to a universal Over-Soul. According to Emerson, God exists both within each individual and as a unifying whole. In his essay "The Over-Soul," he explains this concept:

> [W]ithin man is the soul of the whole; the wise silence; the universal beauty, to which every part and particle is equally related; the eternal ONE. And this deep power in which we exist, and whose beatitude is all accessible to us, is not only

self-sufficing and perfect in every hour, but the act of seeing and the thing seen, the seer and the spectacle, the subject and the object, are one. We see the world piece by piece, as the sun, the moon, the animal, the tree; but the whole, of which these are the shining parts, is the soul.[15]

Emerson also relied upon Kant's theory of how knowledge was acquired. In his writings on reason, Kant distinguished between "Practical Reason," knowledge acquired through observation and logical deduction, and "Pure Reason," knowledge that is not acquired through the senses, such as intuitive perceptions and flashes of insight. The latter form, which Emerson referred to as simply "Reason," formed the basis of Transcendental philosophy.

Reason, the knowledge that comes by intuition, was, in Emerson's view, the highest form of knowledge. Therefore, according to Transcendentalism, the most profound knowledge comes from the self, not from God or the world. The Transcendentalists believed that self-knowledge was the ultimate purpose of life. If every person were to acquire self-knowledge, they speculated, the problems of the world would be solved.

This faith in the self was an important aspect not only of Transcendentalism, but of Romanticism as a whole. Romantic writers, instead of seeking truth in society or God, turned inward and examined the human soul. Even the Romantic exploration of nature was often not a study of nature for its own sake, but a way to gain a better understanding of the self. The work of Poe exemplifies the Romantic belief that the internal world is the source of knowledge. In many of Poe's stories, the protagonists are destroyed by their attempts to seek truth in the material world instead of in the human imagination.

BROOK FARM: AN EXPERIMENT IN TRANSCENDENTALISM

Although Transcendentalism was mostly concerned with ideas, some adherents tried to put these ideas into action through the construction of utopian communities. Founded in 1841 by George and Sophia Ripley, Brook Farm, the most prestigious of these communities, attempted to create an environment in which intellectual and manual labors were integrated. George Ripley describes the goals of Brook Farm as

to combine the thinker and the worker, as far as possible, in the same individual; to guarantee the highest mental freedom by providing all with labor adapted to their tastes and talents, and securing to them the fruits of their industry; to do away with the necessity of menial services by opening the benefits of education and the profits of labor to all; and thus to prepare a society of liberal, intelligent, and cultivated persons whose relations with each other would permit a more simple and wholesome life than can be led amidst the pressure of our competitive institutions.[14]

The agricultural community took root on 170 acres of farmland in West Roxbury, an area outside of Boston, Massachusetts. A member could purchase a share for $500 and receive either free tuition in the community's school or five percent annual interest and one year's board in return for 300 days of labor. Labor consisted of teaching, farming, working in manufacturing shops or on the buildings, domestic duties, and planning cooperative recreation projects. Members were encouraged to engage in both intellectual and manual tasks.

In its early years, the experiment thrived, drawing as many as 4,000 guests, some of whom traveled from places as distant as Cuba and the Philippines to take part in the Brook Farm school. However, the financial difficulties that plagued the community for much of its existence eventually caused the group to disband in 1847.

While Brook Farm reflected the Transcendentalist values of self-reliance, the interrelationship between man and nature, and the rejection of materialism, the community faced scathing criticism from the most prominent Transcendentalist. For Emerson, communal living was dependent upon a sacrifice of individuality. Emerson wrote that "to join [Brook Farm] would be to traverse all my long trumpeted theory, and the instinct which spoke from it, that one man is a counterpoise to a city,—that a man is stronger than a city, that his solitude is more prevalent and beneficent than the concert of crowds."[15]

Another conspicuous critic of Brook Farm was Hawthorne, who was briefly a member of the community. Describing Brook Farm in a letter in 1841, Hawthorne called it "such a delectable way of life [that] has never been seen on earth."[16] However, less than a year later, Hawthorne left Brook Farm in disgust, having concluded that utopian experiments were doomed because they attempted to deny human nature. In his novel *The Blithedale Romance* (1852), Hawthorne satirizes Brook Farm by portraying a communal lifestyle as one that eventually breeds distrust, competition, and deception. A disillusioned member of Hawthorne's fictional community of Blithedale says, "I suddenly found myself possessed by a mood of disbelief in moral beauty or heroism, and a conviction of the folly of attempting to benefit the world."[17]

Ultimately, Hawthorne was unable to accept Brook Farm and its Transcendental philosophy because of his conviction that all people possess a tendency to sin. According to critic Heather O'Toole, Hawthorne's rejection of Transcendentalism was a result of his "belief that at the core of every individual's soul there is some innate evil, some deep down rottenness which prevents any person from achieving absolute, genuine goodness. This evil manifests itself in the form of . . . self-interest, passion, and obsession, and cleverly masks itself with deception."[18]

But Hawthorne was not the only writer to question Transcendentalism's idealism and the spirit of optimism that characterized the Romantic movement in general. Three Romantic writers—Hawthorne, Melville, and Poe—came to be called Anti-Transcendentalists or Negative Romantics because they were unable to accept one of Romanticism's main tenets: a faith in the innate goodness of man and of the world.

THE DECLINE OF ROMANTICISM

The commencement of the Civil War in 1861 caused an abrupt end to Romanticism. At that time the Romantic impulse gave way to a tempering of idealism and a desire to portray society more realistically. The Romantic emphasis on thought and emotion seemed ineffectual in a world that was experiencing dramatic social change.

However, the movement achieved great things, from both a social and literary standpoint. Perhaps its most important social achievement was to create an awareness of the injustices of slavery. Some of the lesser known writers of the period, such as poet John Greenleaf Whittier, launched a direct attack on slavery. In addition, widely read works such as Frederick Douglass's *Narrative of the Life of an American Slave* (1845) and Harriet Beecher Stowe's *Uncle Tom's Cabin* (1852) marked the emergence of an abolitionist passion that would escalate into the Civil War.

Thoreau was also a contributor to the antislavery movement. In 1846, he refused to pay his poll tax because he objected to his money being used to indirectly support slavery. Thoreau was put in jail and released the next morning when an anonymous person paid the tax against his will. His night in jail inspired him to write the essay "Civil Disobedience," in which he claims that it is morally necessary to resist unjust laws. Thoreau's philosophy of non-violent resistance formed the basis of the civil rights movement of the 1960s led by Martin Luther King Jr.

Above all, Romanticism was known for its literary achievement. At no other time in history have so many significant works of literature been published in such a brief span of time. *Moby-Dick*, one of the most renowned books written during that period, set the standard for the great American novel, a standard that would inspire some of the great novels of the twentieth century. American Romanticism also established the United States as a country with a unique and powerful literary tradition. Following this era, no one could write, as Scottish minister Sydney Smith had in 1820, "In the four quarters of the globe, who reads an American book?"[19]

NOTES

1. Ralph Waldo Emerson, "The American Scholar," an oration given to the Phi Beta Kappa Society at Harvard College in Cambridge, Massachusetts, August 31, 1837.

2. Larzer Ziff, *Literary Democracy: The Declaration of Cultural Independence in America.* New York: Viking, 1981, p. xiii.

3. Nathaniel Hawthorne, quoted in Michael Davitt Bell, *The Development of American Romance: The Sacrifice of Relation.* Chicago: University of Chicago Press, 1980, p. 7.

4. Deborah L. Madsen, *Allegory in America: From Puritanism to Postmodernism.* New York: St. Martin's Press, 1996, p. 94.

5. Ralph Waldo Emerson, "The Poet," *Essays, Second Series,* 1884.

6. Robert Penn Warren, Cleanth Brooks, and R.W.B. Lewis, *American Literature: The Makers and the Making.* New York: St. Martin's Press, 1973. Reprinted in *Romanticism: Critical Essays in American Literature.* New York: Garland Publishing, 1986, p. 5.

7. Walt Whitman, http://www.liglobal.com/walt/waltbio.html.

8. Kathryn VanSpanckeren, "An Outline of American Literature: The Romantic Period, 1820–1860: Fiction," wysiwyg://60/http://odur.let.rug.nl/~usa/LIT/ch4_p1.htm.

9. Ralph Waldo Emerson, *Uncollected Writings: Essays, Addresses, Poems, Reviews and Letters by Ralph Waldo Emerson.* New York: 1912, p. 32–33.

10. Frederick Ives Carpenter, *Emerson Handbook.* New York: Hendricks House, 1953. Reprinted in Brian M. Barbour, ed., *American Transcendentalism: An Anthology of Criticism.* Notre Dame: University of Notre Dame, 1973, p. 30.

11. Warren, Brooks, and Lewis, *Romanticism: Critical Essays in American Literature,* p. 13.

12. Rex J. Burbank and Jack B. Moore, eds., *The Literature of the American Renaissance.* Columbus, OH: Charles E. Merrill, 1969, p. 20.

13. Ralph Waldo Emerson, *Essays, First Series,* 1841.

14. George Ripley, quoted in George Hochfield, "New England Transcendentalism," *American Literature to 1900* (ed. Marcus Cunliffe). London: Barrie & Jenkins, 1973. Reprinted in *Critical Essays on American Transcendentalism* (eds. Philip F. Gura and Joel Myerson). Boston: G.K. Hall & Co., 1982, p. 466.

15. Ralph Waldo Emerson, quoted in Hochfield, "New England Transcendentalism," p. 467.

16. Nathaniel Hawthorne, "A Letter from Brook Farm (1841)," *The American Nation: A History of the United States Online,* http://longman.awl.com/garraty/primarysource_11_1.htm.

17. Nathaniel Hawthorne, *The Blithedale Romance,* p. 94.

18. Heather O'Toole, "The Blackness of Men's Souls: Why Nathaniel Hawthorne Could Not Embrace Transcendentalism," p. 1, http://www.bridgewater.edu/philo/philo96/otoole.

19. Sydney Smith, quoted in Keijo Virtanen, "The American Revolution—an .HTML project," wysiwyg://24/http://odur.let.rug.nl/~usa/E/identity/philos01.htm.

CHAPTER 1

Defining American Romanticism

American Romanticism

America During the Period of Romanticism

Rex J. Burbank and Jack B. Moore

Rex J. Burbank is the author of several books on American literature, including works of criticism on Thornton Wilder and Sherwood Anderson. Jack B. Moore, who teaches English at the University of South Florida, is a frequent contributor to print magazines, newspapers, and journals. He is the author of books on W.E.B. Du Bois, Joe DiMaggio, and other famous figures. The following selection was excerpted from the introduction to Burbank's and Moore's anthology entitled *The Literature of the American Renaissance*. In this excerpt, the authors describe the political, economic, and social climate of America during the era of Romanticism.

The writers associated with the so-called Romantic period of American literature matured and worked in a constantly growing nation whose conflicts were basically internal. Most historians feel that the conclusion of the War of 1812 terminated any vestigial status as colony the country might have had. The westward, technological, and urban expansion that marked our emergence as a world power coincided with a flowering in literary art possibly unmatched until the cultural renaissance of post-World War I America.

Historically, the period spans the presidencies of James Monroe, John Quincy Adams, Andrew Jackson, Martin Van Buren, William Henry Harrison, John Tyler, James Polk, Zachary Taylor, Millard Fillmore, Franklin Pierce (whose campaign biography Nathaniel Hawthorne wrote), James Buchanan, and Abraham Lincoln. Monroe (Presidential term, 1817–1825) was the last of the Virginia patricians, landed gentry who seemed on the surface at least to be aristocratic gentlemen. Jackson (1829–1837) represents—part in myth,

Excerpted from Rex J. Burbank and Jack B. Moore, eds., introduction to *The Literature of the American Renaissance* (Columbus, OH: Charles E. Merrill, 1969.) Reprinted with permission from the authors.

part in fact—the President who made possible an era of the common man in politics, and the shrewd, Federalistic, mobocratic manipulator whose job-seeking adherents turned the inaugural into a back-country brawl. Jackson's general popularity underscored the appeal of the common touch in American politics and demonstrated the significance of the West as a regional force. Later presidents such as "Old Tippecanoe" W.H. Harrison and "Old Rough and Ready" Zachary Taylor were faint duplications of the Jacksonian image. Harrison's campaign managers emphasized that his home was a "Log Cabin" without explaining that this was simply a name for Harrison's plantation.

GROWTH AND PROSPERITY

Generally the country grew and prospered, though growth was uneven and periodically there were serious recessions, the worst being the panic of 1837. In New England agricultural failure was not uncommon, and rural areas in both Maine and Vermont suffered population losses. Some religious sects, intellectuals, and a few artisans, dismayed by the country's material prosperity coupled with what seemed spiritual decay and pervasive tastelessness (maybe symbolized by Jackson's purchase of spittoons for the White House costing $12.50 each), and disheartened by periodic depressions, began a number of utopian communities. Brook Farm is perhaps the best known experiment. There Hawthorne met in his words "a transcendental heifer belonging to Miss Margaret Fuller" and learned "that a man's soul may be buried and perish under a dungheap . . . just as well under a pile of money." At Bronson Alcott's Fruitlands, the utopians were so humane they would not use candles made from animal fat. And there were also the Oneida Community, the True Inspiration Society, New Harmony, and others. Over 100 such communities had a combined population of over 100,000. While most of these experiments in communal living and high thinking failed, a few such as the Oneida and Amana communities lived into the twentieth century. Most showed the same impulse that characterized much intellectual life in the nineteenth century: a dissatisfaction with the material values of a fast-growing American economy, and an attempt to bring life under saner human control.

Individualized control in an America bent upon size and speed was difficult to achieve, except perhaps in the life of the mind. The country was growing too rapidly. By 1860 its population was over 31 million, more than that of Great Britain and almost as much as the population of Germany and France. In the decade between 1820 and 1830, Alabama, Arkansas, and Mississippi all doubled their populations. In 1840, Illinois had three times as many people as in 1830. Michigan had seven times as many for the same years. Much of the increase was in city population. Between 1800 and 1860 the number of townsfolk increased twenty-four times, the rural population only quadrupled. By 1820 Pittsburgh already had an air-pollution problem. New York City grew from 123,000 inhabitants in 1820 to over half a million in 1850. Intelligent city planning did not grow with the population: one writer said "Adam and Eve were created and placed in a garden. Cities are a result of the Fall." But the fall seemed fortunate to thousands lured to the city by the American dream of prosperity and, for other reasons, to Walt Whitman, our first great city poet.

Transportation and communication shortened distances for people and goods, even as westward expansion increased. The Erie Canal, completed in 1825, was only one of many Eastern canals constructed by optimistic state governments that wanted a piece of the present and future prosperity. In the late '20's and early '30's railroad construction began, more in the East than in the South. By 1840 railway mileage totalled a tidy 2,818 miles. By 1860 mileage had increased—mostly in the East and West—to 30,000 miles. In 1869 the last spike was driven at Promontory Point, Utah, completing the railroad linking Mid- and Far-West. Steamboats carrying passengers and trade increased almost sixfold between 1820 and 1860. Trade outside the country increased also. In 1853–1854 Commodore Matthew C. Perry's steam-propelled ships helped open Japan to Occidental trade for virtually the first time. So the period produced many "Passages to India" in the symbolic sense, and fostered great movement and great hope. [*Passage to India* is the title of a book of poems written by American Romantic writer Walt Whitman.] Nothing moved much faster than a message over the telegraphic machine, perfected in the late 1830's by Samuel F.B. Morse. And perhaps nothing was more hopeful than the movement west—to California perhaps, where gold-fever hit in the late '40's. Of course not everyone was enthralled with miles of railways or telegraph lines: when the telegraph from Maine to Texas is completed, Henry David Thoreau said, we may discover that "Maine and Texas . . . have nothing important to communicate."

Expansion brought the sections into close connection and competition with each other, not simply economically, but in conflicting ways of life. The regional rivalries of the period met irresistibly in the issues of states' rights and slavery, which the South increasingly defended and the North increasingly attacked. Even the war with Mexico in 1846, which many of the New England intellectuals opposed, was interpreted as resulting from sectional rivalry, for it was seen as an attempt to spread slave territory. Ralph Waldo Emerson attacked the unjustness of the war in his "Ode" to Channing: "Go, blindworm, go, / Behold the famous States / Harrying Mexico / With rifle and with knife!" Thoreau was jailed for refusing to pay taxes to support the war. James Russell Lowell's Birdofredum Sawin made clear the war's inhumanity in his own ironic brand of "Logic": killing Mexicans wasn't any worse than slaughtering pigs, and anyway the Mexicans were like Negroes, "An' kickin' colored folks about, you know, 's kind o' national."

Lowell and John Greenleaf Whittier wrote abolitionist journalism and poetry, and even Henry Wadsworth Longfellow published a volume of anti-slavery poems. The so-called "safety-valve" of westward expansion could not divert the attention of writers and politicians and public from the growing sectional antagonism that found perhaps its chief outlet in the slave problem. In 1831 the American Anti-Slavery Society was formed, and William Garrison founded the *Liberator.* After the War with Mexico, abolitionist writers and anti-slavers directed their concern to the notorious Fugitive Slave Act of 1850, which permitted the forced return of runaway Negroes from free states. *Uncle Tom's Cabin* began its long history in 1851. The Kansas-Nebraska compromise of 1854 culminated in one of the bloodiest popularity contests in American history, the "Kansas War" of 1856, where each side on the slave question seemed convinced that violence was compatible with self-determination in deciding the slave or free state issue. Compromise no longer worked. Daniel Webster had spoken for compromise in 1850 and Whittier wrote about him, "All else is gone; from those great eyes / The soul has fled; / When faith is lost, when honor dies, / The man is dead!" In 1856 there was death in Kansas and near-death in the Senate, where Representative Preston Brooks canewhipped Senator Charles Sumner over the issues of slavery and state's rights. The years are drenched with now-legendary names involved in events all too real. In 1857 Roger B. Taney delivered the majority opinion in the Dred Scott case, seemingly supporting the legality of slavery. In 1859 John Brown dissented and raided Harper's Ferry.

A STRUGGLE FOR RIGHTS

Other explosive issues built up during the period. Emerson was not alone in seeing slave-chains of a different sort in the North. The rights of labor unions had supposedly been affirmed as early as 1842, but labor was only beginning its long struggle to guarantee decent working conditions and to protect women and children from harsh labor practices—from the twelve-hour day for ten-year-olds, from wages of a dollar a week, from company houses containing one store and twenty-five families.

The ladies of Lynn, Massachusetts, who struck against their textile industry bosses in 1860 were treated more seriously as workers than as women: woman's suffrage and equal legal and social rights for women were not yet serious causes. Amelia Bloomer's invention of pants for women (bloomers) won laughs and some sympathy from male supremacists. The period's greatest female intellect, Margaret Fuller, still feared the enlightened New England society she was returning to with her young Italian husband and her once-illegitimate child.

Still, women's rights were an issue of the age, part of the continuing attempt in America to define the rights of man and woman, to explore and not just to limit the physical and intellectual range and scope of Americans. Slavery, industrialization, urbanization, states' rights, exploration, regionalism, labor all offered problems for the nation to confront. The writers were involved with these problems and with matters of craft too, for they were to explore the form and content of art, to investigate how best to shape through art, man's relationship to man, to the universe, to nature and beauty, to real and symbolic good and evil.

Romantic Writers See the World as an Organic Whole

Richard Harter Fogle

Literary scholar Richard Harter Fogle, author of
several works of criticism on American Romanticism, is the editor of a literary anthology entitled
The Romantic Movement in American Writing. The
following selection was taken from Fogle's introduction to the anthology. According to Fogle, the most
significant characteristic of American Romanticism
is a new vision of the world that considers everything as alive, interrelated, and meaningful.

The chief characteristics of the American Romantic movement, seen purely as an imaginative and literary occurrence, are vitality and springtime freshness. One needs to
remember at the same time that this movement represents a
second American spring, a reflowering or, as literary critic
F.O. Matthiessen notably put it, an "American Renaissance."
Such men as Ralph Waldo Emerson and Nathaniel Hawthorne were products of many generations of native culture,
and their Puritan forebears from the first placed tremendous
emphasis upon literary and humanist learning.

Among those writers we may fairly call Romantic, the
main currents flow directly through Emerson, Henry David
Thoreau, and Walt Whitman; more diversely though not less
powerfully in Hawthorne, Edgar Allan Poe, and Herman ›
Melville; less perceptibly in Henry Wadsworth Longfellow,
John Greenleaf Whittier, Oliver Wendell Holmes, and James
Russell Lowell; and in Sidney Lanier through a different and
Southern landscape. The stream has a similar source and
end, but it is the Chattahoochee in Lanier, not the Concord
nor the Aroostook. Time has altered our perspective of the
American Romantics. Those who once reigned supreme,

Excerpted from Richard Harter Fogle, ed., introduction to *The Romantic Movement in American Writing* (New York: Odyssey Press, 1966). Reprinted with permission from the estate of the author.

and seemed to stand in the center of American literature and life, are now diminished and peripheral. The great Brahmins—Longfellow, Whittier, Holmes, and Lowell—have lost their worshippers, and for a time were indeed objects not of reverence but of ridicule. It is certain that they belong in the second rank; the verdict of criticism is just, and is quite unlikely to shift again. Yet we have reached an era when, this side idolatry, we can once more appreciate their genuine gifts and substantial contributions to American literature.

ORIGINS OF AMERICAN ROMANTICISM

To account for American Romantic literature of the nineteenth century it is usual to suggest a variety of cultural, political, religious, and social causes. There is the great breakup of New England Calvinism to consider, a spiritual logjam whose disappearance enfranchised the literary imagination. The Puritan temperament and psychology remained, but were no longer imprisoned in dogma. Out of Calvinism came Unitarianism and then transcendentalism, more hospitable to literary growth. Correspondingly the rise of physical and political nationalism fostered the rise of an American literature to match. (The call for the American literary genius was loud even in the very early 1800's.) The expansion of the nation and the receding continental frontier were physical, material symbols of the Romantic craving for indefinite growth and development. The population of the United States increased from less than 10,000,000 in 1820 to over 31,000,000 in 1860, an explosion perhaps not as massive and critical as in the world today but greater in proportion, while the expansion in territory was still more impressive. Material greatness called out, not in vain, for imaginative greatness to match it and make it intelligible. This was in part a matter simply of an ambitious nation's pride, but more deeply there was the enormous need of the American mind to find its home, to clothe its nakedness, to populate empty space. "The land was ours before we were the land's," as Robert Frost in our own time still found it necessary to say. To fill this need involved some overstraining, in Emerson, Thoreau, Whitman, Melville; but the results could be well-nigh miraculous, as in *Moby-Dick*.

The expansive idealism of the American Romantic Movement was far from exclusively native. It owed much to the Romanticism of England and of Germany, a movement per-

vasive in Europe from the late eighteenth century on. The
German philosophers Herder, Kant, Fichte, and Schelling
had transformed the smooth-running mechanical world of
Sir Isaac Newton and the passivist material psychology of
Thomas Hobbes and John Locke. With a kindred impulse in
England, Coleridge and William Wordsworth asserted new
and vital potentialities in nature and the mind of man. The
influence of Samuel Taylor Coleridge (1772–1834), particularly in such prose works as *Biographia Literaria* and *Aids to
Reflection,* was dominant in the most advanced American literary criticism and metaphysics; it had much to say to Emerson, Poe, Hawthorne, and Melville, as to the transcendentalists generally. Those who read the best American journals of
the Golden Age of the 1840's will find Coleridge's traces
everywhere. Emerson's good friend Thomas Carlyle, with
his strenuous idealism and ethical message, had a nearly
equal impact. Wordsworth's poetry was the norm for the
imaginative vision of nature as early as William Cullen
Bryant, "the American Wordsworth," and held its position
until the 1850's. Among the other English Romantic poets
and novelists, Sir Walter Scott and Lord Byron held sway in
the aristocratic and chivalric South (Mark Twain laid the
Civil War at the door of Sir Walter), and had some effect upon
the young Poe. Poe later on got much also from Coleridge and
Percy Shelley, as was true of both Hawthorne and Melville.

What is Romanticism? Perhaps no single definition of it is
at the same time broad enough to cover the whole ground
and particular enough for significant application. But it nevertheless exists, and can be described and exemplified. Tra-
ditionally the Romantic emphasizes the potentialities of
things, especially things that have gone hitherto unnoticed
or despised. Wordsworth concludes his "Ode on Intimations
of Immortality" by asserting that

> To me the meanest flower that blows can give
> Thoughts that do often lie too deep for tears,

and William Blake has the gift

> To see the world in a grain of sand,
> And Heaven in a wild flower.

THE PHILOSOPHY OF ORGANICISM

The center of Romanticism, however, lies in a new and different vision, in which everything is alive, related, and mean-

ingful. This involves "organicism," according to which all reality is organically and vitally unified. Organicism is not a metaphysical or poetical idea alone; it rose as a distinct conception with the rise of the biological sciences in the latter part of the eighteenth century. The old physics and mathematics emphasized abstraction and analytical classification in order to produce accurate and universally applicable results, but now the problem and the hope arose of analyzing life itself—the living cell, the living body—in biology, botany, and organic chemistry. The process of synthesis was found to be as basic as the process of analysis. Full realization of organic unity and life does not, however, lie within the competence of science, which must still abstract and classify to obtain its results. It cannot deal with the uniqueness of things, which is left to the imagination of the artist, whether he be poet, painter, musician, or, as in the case of Emerson, philosopher.

The most complex relationships were now seen to be organic rather than merely mechanical; whereas reality had once been figured as a smoothly working watch, a great and orderly machine, the analogy for it now became the growing plant or tree. Along with life itself, the mysterious process of growth stood forth as the central component in creation. Thus all things move, develop, grow, and to cease to grow is death. Reality is not static, but alive, ever moving and changing. And to penetrate into this reality is a gift of the imagination, which alone can relate man to nature, subject to object, the human mind to its external environment. Coleridge, in a famous discussion of imagination, declared that "All objects, as objects, are essentially fixed and dead"; their life, that is, is akin to the life of the subject that beholds, and the relationship is the center of its realization.

From these ideas of organic life and organic growth developed the further notion of organic form. Thus Coleridge, paralleling the German A.W. Schlegel, wrote that "The organic form is innate; it shapes, as it develops itself from within, and its fullness is one and the same with the perfection of its outward form. Such as is the life, such is the form." Mechanical form, on the other hand, is determined from outside: "The form is mechanic when on any given material we impress a predetermined form . . . as when to a mass of wet clay we give whatever shape we wish it to retain when hardened." The relationships in a work of art are then, like the relationships of life, inseparable, and what is revealed to the artist's creative imagination is objectified in a form akin to it. Form and content are not different elements of the work, but, at least ideally speaking, one and the same.

This metaphor of organic form is marvelously tempting and attractive to the critic, the philosopher, and the practitioner of literary and other art. One may say simply that it is the most *interesting* possible view, and the view most conducive to that confidence, affirmation, and desire of celebration that properly belongs to the artist. It is wonderfully ap-

MELVILLE AND ORGANICISM

For the reader predisposed to feel that "form" means "classical form," with a controlling geometric structure, *Moby-Dick* is and will remain an aesthetically unsatisfying experience. One needs only to compare it with *The Scarlet Letter,* published a year and a half earlier, to see how non-classical it is. . . .

To go from *The Scarlet Letter* to *Moby-Dick is* to move from the Newtonian world-as-machine to the Darwinian world-as-organism. In the older cosmology the key concepts had been law, balance, harmony, reason; in the newer, they became origin, process, development, growth. Concurrently biological images arose to take the place of the older mechanical analogies: growing plants and life forms now symbolized cosmic ultimates better than a watch or the slow-turning rods and gears of an eighteenth-century orrery. . . .

The matter of *Moby-Dick is* the organic land-sea world where life forms move mysteriously among the elements. The dynamic of the book is the organic mind-world of Ishmael whose sensibility rhythmically agitates the flux of experience. The controlling structure of the book is an organic complex of rhetoric, symbols, and interfused units. There is no over-reaching formal pattern of literary art on which *Moby-Dick* is a variation. To compare it with the structure of the Elizabethan play, or the classical epic, or the modern novel is to set up useful analogies rather than congruous models. It is a free form that fuses as best it can innumerable devices from many literary traditions, including contemporary modes of native expression. In the last analysis, if one must have a prototype, here is an intensively heightened rendition of the logs, journals, and histories of the Anglo-American whaling tradition.

Walter E. Bezanson, *Moby-Dick: Centennial Essays* (ed. Tyrus Hillway and Luther S. Mansfield), 1953.

propriate to the actual richness, complexity, and vitality of
the creative process in art, too full for the artist himself to follow, and too swift in its working. A very short poem may take
a great many words to describe discursively and analytically,
and remain unexhausted in the face of our utmost efforts—
which is fortunate. Poe, in some respects the most analytical
and unsentimental of critics, who would reduce meaning in
art to conscious and calculated effect, is unable to account
for the vital stuff of his own poems and stories. Or, as Emerson asks of the creative process in "The Problem,"

> Know'st thou what wove yon woodbird's nest
> Of leaves, and feathers from his breast?
> Or how the fish outbuilt her shell,
> Painting with morn each annual cell?
> Or how the sacred pine-tree adds
> To her old leaves new myriads?
> Such and so grew these holy piles,
> Whilst love and terror laid the tiles.

The various qualities which have from time to time been
attributed to Romanticism can all be related to the large concept of organicism. . . . Cultivation of the sense of wonder, for
example, follows naturally from the richness and complexity
of the organic vision, and the sense of potentiality and the aspiration for infinitude are concomitants of organic growth,
which in itself has no logical limits. A cardinal tenet of Romanticism is the presence of the unusual within the usual, as
it is revealed to the imagination; Wordsworth and Coleridge
again and again enounced this principle, and the Americans
followed them. This search for a hidden wonder involves
more than literary purposes; it is concerned with democracy,
with social justice, with love and charity, with the general
welfare of the modern mind and modern society. For true
democracy is only possible when we perceive the value of
our fellows, however alien or insignificant their surface appearance, and this value in turn is visible only when we see
that they are like ourselves, in vital relationship. Without this
sense there is no meaning in social progress and reform.
Further, the Romantics believed that the modern mind itself
was in danger, from incomplete and perverted values, from
a disproportionate emphasis upon some aspects of reality to
the exclusion of others. The utilitarian, the materialist, sees
and in consequence lives in a dead world.

Individualism, another Romantic characteristic, is thus
not to be confused with egotism and conceit. One respects

the potentialities in oneself as one respects those of others. If one can see the world in a grain of sand, if the structure of a crystal is the structure of totality, then the self too is a microcosm of the macrocosm, an entity of rich and inexhaustible interest. "Trust thyself; every heart vibrates to that iron string," exhorted Emerson. Whitman says,

> I celebrate myself, and sing myself,
> And what I assume you shall assume,
> For every atom belonging to me as good belongs to you.

The self-reliant Thoreau retires to Walden not to isolate but to fulfill himself, and in so doing to show others the true richness of human experience.

Romanticists are idealists; they will not limit themselves to the evidence of the senses or to the reality of matter alone. They will not deny the existence of God for the sake of their own freedom, for the denial would impoverish, not enrich, and God is the extension of their aspirations to infinity. At the same time, in a world of organic unity the reality of the spirit is not separate from the reality of the senses, and Nature is a symbol and a manifestation of the divine, as it is also of the human.

American Romanticism Expresses a Belief in Self-Reliance

Tremaine McDowell

Professor and literary critic Tremaine McDowell contends in the following selection, excerpted from the introduction to *The Romantic Triumph: American Literature from 1830 to 1860*, that the American Romantic movement was characterized by a trust in humanity and in the individual. According to McDowell, the Romantic writers sought self-reliance as individuals and as members of a newly independent nation.

"We will walk with our own feet; we will work with our own hands; we will speak with our own minds." In these bold words Ralph Waldo Emerson gave voice to the pervasive self-reliance of the Romantic generation in France and Germany, England and the United States. If any one belief can be called central to the Romantic Movement in America, it is this trust in mankind and in the individual.

The Renaissance, the Reformation, and the Age of Reason had set in motion influences which in the late eighteenth and the early nineteenth century culminated in this new respect for the human race and for every man. In warfare, common men equipped with gunpowder had long since demonstrated their equality with gentlemen in armor. In commerce, middle-class traders had broken the monopolies of nobles and monarchs. In government, the divine right of kings was everywhere challenged by the inalienable rights of men: their right to revolution; their right to found a state through delegation of their own innate authority; their right to life, liberty, and the pursuit of happiness. In religion, God was envisioned less as an unlimited and irresponsible monarch and more as a reasonable and benevolent father, to

Reprinted with permission of Simon & Schuster, Inc. from *The Romantic Triumph: American Literature from 1830 to 1860*, Revised Edition by Tremaine McDowell. Copyright ©1949 by Macmillan Publishing Company, renewed 1977.

whom his children may have direct access without the mediation of Christ or clergy. In philosophy, the idealists contended that truth for each man is that fraction of ultimate truth which he himself comprehends.

Both cause and result of these ideas was the new and vastly influential belief that man is fundamentally good rather than naturally evil. From this confidence that the individual is worthy to grow and expand came confidence that he should and will expand and that, since individuals form society, society will thereby be improved. Thus was born the theory of progress for men and for man—a theory not original to the United States but commonly accepted by American Romanticists as a tenet of the American faith.

On these foundations, the Romantic generation built their doctrine of individualism. Even though they commonly acknowledged the omnipotence of the Deity, they were moving steadily away from a God-centered order toward a universe centered in man. Ultimate values were in certain instances still derived from authority and tradition, but more often they were those values which the individual found welcome to himself. To be explicit, beauty was for Edgar Allan Poe those particular aspects of universal beauty by which he himself was moved. Goodness for Emerson was to establish union with the Over-Soul, then to refuse all good models and to go alone. In short, life came into sharpest focus for the Romanticist when it was interpreted in the terms of his own personality: "Nothing is at last sacred but the integrity of your own mind."

ROMANTICISM AND THE COMMON MAN

Out of this concern with the individual arose one of the numerous paradoxes of the Romantic Triumph. On the one hand, Romanticists made much of the common man, who in the United States was still overwhelmingly agrarian. John Greenleaf Whittier sang of farmers, lumbermen, and shoemakers, of migrants and the poor. Emerson learned wisdom from strong-natured farmers and Henry David Thoreau listened to rude Yankees whom he exuberantly described as "fuller of talk and rare adventure in sun and rain, than a chestnut is of meat; greater men than Homer, or Chaucer, or Shakespeare, only they never got time to say so." Professor Henry Wadsworth Longfellow of Harvard College spoke kindly of a village blacksmith, while in the West the folk immortalized Sweet Betsy from Pike [a folk song about the California gold rush]. On the other hand, Romantics glorified the superman. Poe revived the legend of Tamerlane the conqueror; Emerson praised Napoleon as the apotheosis of "those who have not" (then demolished him as a man deficient in moral sense) Herman Melville created in Captain Ahab a gigantic exponent of Romantic rebellion and egomania; and the frontier added Mike Fink, Davy Crockett, and Andy Jackson to the nation's gallery of earth-shaking heroes.

But even the most egocentric Romanticists could exist as individuals only in relation to that which lay outside them. Inevitably, then, they projected themselves into contemporary society. Nearest to each man was his own state and his own section. Thus young Augustus Baldwin Longstreet associated himself with the Georgia frontier; John Pendleton Kennedy and William Gilmore Simms identified themselves with the South. Daniel Webster was long the unofficial president of New England; Whittier, the self-appointed chronicler of Yankee legend; James Russell Lowell, the recorder of Yankee dialect; Oliver Wendell Holmes, the poet-laureate of the Brahmin caste. And Nathaniel Hawthorne announced that New England was quite as large a lump of earth as his heart could encompass.

Of the Romanticists who identified themselves with their own section, the noisiest were that third of the nation who lived beyond the Alleghenies. The West was still so young that it expressed itself almost wholly in popular song and folk-tale. Western song was couched always in the experience and often in the dialect of the Great Migration, while every folk hero raucously announced that he was the essence and the acme of the frontier. The first reactions of New England to the West were conservative and therefore unfavorable. But Thoreau saw in the frontier that virility and "wildness" which he sought ("We need a tonic of wildness"). After the West produced Jackson, the East began to realize that the land beyond the mountains was, in Hawthorne's extravagant phrase, a land "on which the damned shadow of Europe had not fallen." Lowell declared that nature had shaped Abraham Lincoln out of fresh clay from the unexhausted West, with "nothing of Europe here." Emerson traveled widely through the new states, braving subzero temperatures, indifferent food, and barbarous sleeping-quarters (he once spent the night "wreathed in legs" on the deck of a steamboat) that he might talk with and to those rugged exponents of self-trust, the frontiersmen. For him the West in its best moments was America.

When expansive individualists found the resources of any one section inadequate to express their ego, they identified themselves with the American republic. The result was self-reliance in national terms—the healthy self-assurance of a youthful society on the make. Since it was also at many points a Christian society, Americans announced that God had underwritten their self-trust. "We are the pioneers of the world," Herman Melville declared in a moment of optimism. "God has predestined, mankind expects, great things from our race; and great things we feel in our souls. The most of the nations must soon be in our rear. We are . . . the advance guard, sent on through the wilderness of untried things."

THE RISE OF NATIONALISM

Because the establishment of the American republic was an experiment and an adventure, the national faith voiced by Melville long animated its citizens and set them apart as a chosen race, destined to high achievement. This faith had earlier supported the rebellious colonists through unheroic ordeals of the Revolution; and this aspiration had guided the mutually suspicious states into a federal union. In the decades from 1830 to 1860, nationalism made itself felt in public affairs in the form of self-reliant expansiveness. A necessary preliminary to the emergence of this dynamic spirit had been the second war with England which gave the American people increased self-respect. Then came the conviction that the American experiment in republican government was a triumphant success and that the native culture which patriots had long but vainly attempted to create by decree was spontaneously emerging. Finally, in the 1840's and the 1850's, the conservatism of earlier years succumbed to a new optimism and the American people, fired by Utopian faith, gave themselves over to innovation and expansion. Abroad, Yankee ships entered every world-port; American trade touched every continent. At home, pioneers pushed across the plains into Oregon; forty-niners swept into California; imperialists laid violent hands on Texas. Meanwhile, national self-trust and the theory of progress so dominated religious, social, and political theory that a President of the United States could declare: "I believe man can be elevated;

man can become more and more endowed with divinity; and as he does, he becomes more God-like in character and capable of governing himself. Let us go on elevating our people, perfecting our institutions, until democracy shall reach such a point of perfection that we can acclaim with truth that the voice of the people is the voice of God."

As prophet of the Romantic generation, Emerson had the high distinction of enunciating our national declaration of intellectual and literary independence. Vague prophecies of the coming intellectual supremacy of America had been written by Freneau, Dwight, and their brother poets; but to none of these early enthusiasts had it been revealed exactly how native thought might be freed from foreign masters; and the American mind had remained "timid, imitative, tame." At length, after Channing had prepared the way, Emerson announced in "The American Scholar" his simple but effective, and universal, formula. Let Americans bring to their thinking and writing the stimulus of Romantic individualism, let them accept the gospel of self-reliance, and "our long day of dependence, our long apprenticeship to the reaming of other lands" will draw to a close. When Poe and Melville, Hawthorne, Thoreau, and Emerson, and the folk of the Western frontier thought with their own minds and spoke in their own words, then a new literature was created. This was the birth (not the renascence) of American letters.

Finally, the Transcendentalists projected themselves into the universe and made themselves one with it and with the Deity. To Emerson the great world was "a mere illustration" of the mind, a mere "externalization of the soul." The two precepts, "Know thyself" and "Study nature," are therefore one. In so far as a man is good, said Emerson, so far he is God. And "the simplest person who in his integrity worships God, becomes God."

American Romanticism Is Humanistic

David Bowers

Literary critic David Bowers is the author of the following selection, excerpted from *Literary History of the United States*. Bowers maintains that the diverse writers of the American Romantic movement—Emerson, Thoreau, Hawthorne, Melville, and Whitman—are unified by a common interest in the problems of humanity. These writers sought to explain the world by gaining a better understanding of man himself.

In quality of style, and particularly in depth of philosophic insight, American literature has not yet surpassed the collective achievement of Ralph Waldo Emerson, Henry David Thoreau, Nathaniel Hawthorne, Herman Melville, and Walt Whitman. Having freed itself in these writers from its earlier tendencies either blindly to imitate or blindly to reject European models, American literature here for the first time sloughed off provincialism, and, by being itself—by saying only what it wanted to say and as it wanted to say it—attained, paradoxically, the rank and quality of world literature, a literature authentic not only in America but everywhere the English tongue is understood. . . .

At first sight, Emerson, Thoreau, Hawthorne, Melville, and Whitman seem to differ from one another more than they agree. For one thing, they are divergent in temperament. Thoreau, Whitman, and—above all—Emerson are prevailingly optimistic. Hawthorne, on the other hand, is at least fatalistic in point of view; while Melville seems to have run the entire emotional gamut from optimism through pessimism to final resignation. Again, all of them differ widely in their choice of subject matter and literary form. Primarily novelists, Hawthorne and Melville are concerned with the psychological and allegorical analysis of certain types of human personality and moral situations; primarily poets and essayists, Emerson, Thoreau, and Whitman focus, each in his own way, upon the underlying relation of man to nature.

Most widely of all, they differ in their interest and capacity for sustained philosophical thought. None of them could be described as interested in philosophical theory for its own sake—not even Emerson, who is less intolerant of abstract reasoning than the rest. But even within these limits their divergency is still great. For although we can find at least traces of a comprehensive philosophical system in Emerson, the traces become progressively more rudimentary in Thoreau, Melville, and Whitman, until at last in Hawthorne they almost disappear.

A COMMON CONCERN

Yet this incommensurability is not absolute. Common to them as to all great writers, is a profound sense of the human predicament, of the questions that beset man as man, and of the relation of these problems to man's defects and potentialities. Their common concern surmounts all differences, as may be seen in Emerson's and Hawthorne's treatment of the problem of evil. When Emerson proclaims the non-existence of evil in an ultimate form and Hawthorne rejects this conception as tragically blind, neither writer is proceeding on the assumption that the problem of evil itself is unreal or trivial. For Hawthorne, as we know, it is the most pressing of all problems, while for Emerson—as the haunting overtones of "Experience" intimate—it is a problem which can be optimistically resolved only after the most desperate of inward struggles and only after attaining a serenity almost stripped of emotion. In other words, the difference between the two lies not in their conception of the importance of the problem but only in their conception of its proper solution.

Common also to all these writers is the framework of ideas within which they seek to understand the problem of man. Even when it provides quite divergent solutions the framework or perspective is in all instances radically humanistic.

Its basic premise is that man is the spiritual center of the universe and that in man alone can we find the clue to nature, history, and ultimately the cosmos itself. Without denying outright the existence either of God or of brute matter, it nevertheless rejects them as exclusive principles of inter-pretation and prefers to explain man and his world so far as possible in terms of man himself. This is expressed most clearly in the transcendentalist principle that the structure of the universe literally duplicates the structure of the indi-vidual self, and that all knowledge therefore begins with self-knowledge. But it is no less evident in the moral earnestness of Hawthorne and Melville, which leads them to dwell ceaselessly upon the allegory of the human soul and to personalize impersonal nature itself as an allegory of hu-man experience. It is because of this, for example, that few

THOREAU'S HUMANISM

We meet Henry David Thoreau's humanism on two lev-els: an immediate level, on which the test of anything is its relevancy to life; and a more submerged one, on which cer-tain basic assumptions in Thoreau's total outlook are found to be operative. The reader of Thoreau encounters the test of rel-evancy to life in every matter he discusses—economics, travel, architecture, government, friendship, religion, commerce, and all, including, of course, literature. Although it is to anticipate somewhat a later discussion, one can illustrate this test in the topic at hand. To Thoreau literature and life are united in an essential concern with human experience, a point of view that is illustrated in many ways. The written word to him is the "most perfect work of human art" because it is "nearest to life itself" and books are greatest if they truly embody life. "We do not learn much from learned books, but from sincere, human books, from frank and honest biographies." His own aim in writing *Walden*, as he states it in the opening pages, embodies, of course, this attitude. That this relevancy is the test is further indicated by the fact that in any disjunction of literature and life Thoreau believes that the life lived is more important than the life written about. We have, for example, his well known autobiographical comment,

> My life hath been the poem I would have writ,
> But I could not both live and utter it.

And again such statements as these: "He is the truest artist whose life is his material"; "The real facts of a poet's life would be of more value to us than any work of his art."

Thoreau's humanism on the deeper level of his basic atti-tudes, his "philosophy," if we can use that term, is a more complicated problem. The fundamental issue is what Thoreau incidents in their plots ever turn out to be wholly fortuitous or to be without symbolic significance for the characters involved in them.

This common perspective is also, in all cases, radically universalized. Its emphasis is almost never upon man as particular—as European, say, or as American—but almost always upon man as universal, upon man as freed from the accidents of time and space as well as from those of birth and talent and reduced to his common humanity. It is apparent not only in Emerson and Thoreau but also in Hawthorne, Melville, and Whitman; none of them even in the

considered reality to be, a recurrent concern throughout his writings. Taking his work as a whole, one can say that reality to Thoreau is the relationship—the creative synthesis—of the self and all outside of self. Thoreau never explicitly defines reality, but in various less direct ways he points to this conclusion. For example, there is his imperative that each person base his life upon reality, as when in the *Walden* chapter "Where I Lived . . ." he urges us "to work and wedge our feet downward through mud and slush of opinion, and prejudice, and delusion and appearance . . . till we come to a hard bottom and rocks in place, which we can call reality, and say, This is, and no mistake . . . ;" What we need is "not a Nilometer but a Realometer. . . ." This feeling for reality is found in much of *Walden*, as for example in the "Conclusion," where he contends that he finds no satisfaction in trying to spring an arch before he has a solid foundation; "there is a solid bottom everywhere." He comes closer to saying what reality is by indicating that the pathway to it involves an examination of self. The journey in the *Week*, the suggested self-analysis in much of the pond symbolism in *Walden*, and most directly in the *Walden* "Conclusion," where the hunting, travel, and exploring images constitute an exhortation to self-searching, all bear witness to this belief. And there are explicit statements here such as "A man must find occasions in himself, it is true" and "Let every one mind his own business and endeavor to be what he was made." Even earlier we find him pointing out that there is a "certain choice energy in every man"; this is "the crank within—the crank after all—the prime mover in all machinery—quite indispensable to all work. Would that we might get our hands on its handle."

E. Earle Stibitz, *Critical Theory in the American Renaissance* (ed. Darrel Abel), 1969.

most concrete and practical moments can ever quite forget that the drama of man is clothed with the aspect of eternity. Thus, for Emerson, the "American Scholar" turns out to be simply "Man Thinking"; while, for Whitman, the song of himself merges imperceptibly into a song of all the "children of Adam," where "every atom belonging to me as good belongs to you." Thus also, in spite of a frequently high degree of individualization, the characters and situations of Hawthorne and Melville are fundamentally impersonal, emerging at their best as a fusion of particular and type but at their worst as types only.

This turning away from the current scientific view of the world and regression under the impetus of European idealism to the Neo-Platonic conception of nature as a living mystery full of signs and portents, revives a conception with which some of the five were already familiar from their reading in the literature of the seventeenth century and of religious mysticism. At the same time, a principle of correspondence is evolved which promises the reconciliation rather than the rejection of science.

Nor can we overestimate the practical importance of this conception from either the literary or the social point of view. In terms of literature, for instance, its construing of nature as inherently symbolic invests the natural faculty of imagination with a new prestige, dissolving the older literary emphasis upon wit, sentiment, and rationality, and preparing the way for the symbolist literature to come. Even more far-reaching are the social implications of the conception. For by postulating, as it does, an identity between the categories of impersonal nature and the categories of human psychology—and thereby also the unity of creation—the conception provides a metaphysical basis for the belief in democratic equality to which the social philosophy of Emerson, Thoreau, and Whitman can and does appeal.

THE IMPORTANCE OF SELF-REALIZATION

The second assumption common to all five writers is the belief that individual virtue and happiness depend upon self-realization, and that self-realization, in turn, depends upon the harmonious reconciliation of two universal psychological tendencies: first, the expansive or self-transcending impulse of the self, its desire to embrace the whole world in the experience of a single moment and to know and become one with that world; and second, the contracting or self-asserting impulse of the individual, his desire to withdraw, to remain unique and separate, and to be responsible only to himself.

The current theory of self as expounded by Samuel Taylor Coleridge and other Europeans was adaptable here, and its importance was more than theoretical because it stated in universal terms the central goal and problem of democracy itself. On the one hand, democracy as a moral and political doctrine implied an ethic of extreme individualism, one which preserved to the individual a maximum degree of freedom and self-expression. On the other hand, the democratic self was divided. There was, first, the conflict between its traditional sense of duty to God and its new-found sense of duty to man. There was, second, the conflict between the duty to self as implied by the concept of liberty and the duty to society as implied by the other two concepts of the revolutionary triad, equality and fraternity. Hence, a doctrine which recognizes the divisions in the self and insists that their reconciliation is necessary for true self-realization defines not only the democratic ethic in general but also the specific hope of democracy that the self can be realized without sacrificing any side of its nature, altruistic as well as egoistic.

There can be no doubt that all five of the writers define the ethical ideal in these terms, although, characteristically, they disagree both on *how* the ideal is to be actualized and on the degree to which it is actualizable. Thus Emerson, Thoreau, and Whitman, who accept its actualization as a real possibility because they have assumed to begin with that the self and the cosmos express one and the same spiritual force, disagree on what specific course of action will convert their inner harmony into an outward fact. For while Emerson and Thoreau believed the harmony can be fully realized by the simple, though paradoxical, expedient of forgetting the world and being true only to oneself, Whitman seems to hold that there is needed an unlimited love of creation as such, a love that will include the self and the world as one.

In contrast to these three stand Hawthorne and Melville, who doubt whether a genuine harmony between the individual and his cosmos is possible at all. For although both assume that the destiny of man is ever to seek such a harmony, they are also deeply convinced that the self and the cosmos are victim to tragic flaws which prevent their ever realizing it. Hawthorne discovers the flaws both in the spiritual pride and spiritual weakness of the individual and in the intractability of his social environment. And Melville identifies them with a defect in the universe at large, symbolized in the inscrutability of the white whale.

But both writers hold that the flaws, in all cases, effectively block a final rapport between the individual and the world. For although the conflict between these two protagonists is sometimes susceptible of an emotional resolution—either by a daemonic assertion of the will, as in Captain Ahab, or by the will's abnegation, as in Hester Prynne and Billy Budd—the resolution is only partial since it is at the cost of eliminating either the world or the self from final moral consideration. In other words, where Emerson, Thoreau, and Whitman discover in the romantic theory of self-realization grounds for ultimate hope, Hawthorne and Melville draw from it only tragic irresolution.

INTUITION AND IMAGINATION

The third assumption common to the five writers is that intuition and imagination offer a surer road to truth than abstract logic or scientific method. It is a corollary to their belief that nature is organic, and corresponds to the technical distinction between the reason as intuition and the understanding as logical analysis. In the specific form of this distinction, the assumption appears frequently in Emerson. But as a general principle underlying both theory and practice it is present in all.

It is illustrated by their emphasis upon introspection—their belief that the clue to outer nature is always to be found in the inner world of individual psychology—and by their constant interpretation of experience as in essence symbolic. For both these stresses presume an organic relationship between the self and the cosmos of which only intuition and imagination can properly take account.

Finally, in terms of the third assumption, all five writers were able to deduce a consequence of immense practical importance not only for their own work but for the subsequent course of American literature as a whole. Not only could the belief in the primacy of imagination be used to justify their own tendency toward the concrete, the metaphorical, and the didactic; it also had the wider implication of attaching greater significance to the craft of literature generally. Once the faculty of imagination is placed on a par with the faculty of reason, the writer as the primary exponent of the imagination acquires an importance in society at least equal to that of the scientist, the philosopher, and the theologian. All equally can then claim to be engaged in the same pursuit: the search for truth.

It is undoubtedly their faith in the imagination and in themselves as practitioners of imagination that enabled Emerson, Thoreau, Hawthorne, Melville, and Whitman to achieve supreme confidence in their own moral and metaphysical insights. It is this also that led them to conceive of the writer as a seer, and thus to exemplify in their attitude toward literature the emphasis upon its responsibility to life which is characteristic of our own day.

American Romanticism Challenged the Values of America

Warren Staebler

Warren Staebler is professor emeritus of English
at Earlham College in Richmond, Indiana. He has
also served as Fulbright-Hays professor of American
literature at the University of Wroclaw in Poland.
In the following selection, excerpted from a speech
given at the International Conference on American
Studies in Budapest, Staebler explains the ways in
which the American Romantics challenged the
culture and values of the United States.

I take originality to mean not just differences but differences
in nature which are immediately apparent. The essential
nature of American Romantic writers which makes them
original is their closeness to the life of the new nation—their
intense consciousness of the principles on which the nation
had been founded, of the ideal it was intended to fulfill. This
was a consciousness which colored not only their lives in
the young society but also the expression of imaginative experience in their writings and the end to which they were
aimed. And it was a consciousness which made them all
sayers of *No*.

In what respects was Edgar Allan Poe a sayer of *No*? First,
in his vision of man and the universe. Poe, viewing the universe as shrouded in dreadful night, saw human beings as
forsaken and moved by dark subliminal forces they were
unable to control to the destruction of themselves and others. The human heart was occupied by "a grim legion of
sepulchral terrors" and life was "much of madness and
more of Sin / [with] Horror the soul of the plot." That Poe
said *No* to such a state of things we know from his poetry. He
sought, in a kind of Platonic desperation, and trusting in an

Excerpted from Warren Staebler's paper, "The Originality of Vision in the American Ro-
mantics," presented at the International Conference in American Studies, Budapest,
April 9–11, 1980. Reprinted in Tibor Frank, ed., *The Origins and Originality of American
Culture* (Budapest: Akadémiai Kiadó, 1984). Reprinted with permission from the author.

"ecstatic prescience," to escape from the ghastliness of it to "the glories that lie beyond the grave" through the creation of supernal beauty in his poems, and through the love of woman to seal his celestial salvation. But more particularly, Poe was a sayer of *No* to America. He rejected the American scene as setting for his tales, he revealed no sense of community in them, he sneered at the idea of an American Literature, and he had only contempt for the principles on which the country was founded. Rather like le Marquis de Sade, he derided the affirmative rationalistic thinkers of the 18th century for their *a priori*, deductive reasoning. Thomas Jefferson, in declaring men to be endowed by their creator with certain inalienable rights, was guilty of "dictating purposes to God." Eighteenth-century philosophers should have defined man according to what he was "always occasionally doing rather than upon the basis of what" they "thought the Deity intended him to do." What man was doing was evil, was wrong, but out of perversity he did it precisely because it was wrong, destroying himself and others. As for the form of government of his native land, Poe scathed it as "a very admirable form of government—for dogs."

HAWTHORNE: A REFORMER OF PURITANISM

Nathaniel Hawthorne accepted the universe and he never renounced, let alone denounced, the society and culture of his native land. And as to its government, he represented it in a diplomatic post abroad. Nevertheless, in various respects, he was a sayer of *No*. In his work he examined not only the nature of the Puritan social and moral order of the 17th century, but also the nature of the 19th. The Puritans of Boston in 1650 were "the most intolerant brood that ever lived," and Hawthorne took shame upon himself for his own forebears, hoping to expiate their guilt. The Puritans, "stern and black-browed," led lives of bleak severity. They were guilty of unrelenting legalism, mercilessly translating private shame and suffering into punitive public exhibition and mortification, as in the case of Hester Prynne of *The Scarlet Letter.* They had strenuous intellects apt for creating systems of theology, which, alas, were only creations of "stupendous impertinence." And they were deficient in understanding all that related to the feeling side of human nature, to what Hawthorne called "the sanctity of the human heart." The Puritans, champions of freedom from the autocratic Stuart King

Charles I, Hawthorne never ceased to admire and praise. But what they had achieved as community was not enough; it was the product of minds that had "imagined and hoped" too little. As for the social system inherited from them, it was wrong in the unjustice of the place it allowed to women, and needed to be reformed. Yet he did not know how. Radical theorists who would make it over according to reason, he had no patience with. The nature of men, and of women, too, needed to be purified, before social renovation could take place. The human heart needed first to be cleansed and altered. In all of this Hawthorne was against that strand of rationalist perfectibility in American culture which in his own day had gotten out of hand in zealous social reformers.

MELVILLE'S CONDEMNATION OF AMERICA

Herman Melville, the third of the great dark Romantics and an admirer of Hawthorne for his saying of *No*, aspired to be himself a black thinker, a thought-diver—one of those who like Shakespeare plunged again and again to the bottom of the sea of unconventional belief and came up with bloodshot eyes. Where evidence of *no-saying* to America is concerned, it is not to *Moby Dick* that one goes to find it. It is in other works that Melville takes America to task for her wrongs and failures. In *Typee*, for example, he censures her unnatural sexual mores by depicting the free behavior of the beautiful-bodied islanders of the South Pacific. But more importantly he condemns the venality of America for not bringing the South Sea islanders to a higher kind of life but only exploiting and extirpating them.

> Let the savages be civilized, but civilize them with benefits and not with evils; and let heathenism be destroyed, but not by destroying the heathen. The Anglo-Saxon hive (sic) have extirpated Paganism from the greater part of the North American continent, but with it they have likewise extirpated the greater portion of the red race.

In *Pierre* and *The Confidence Man*, Melville's targets are American materialism, philistinism, and credulity. The impossibility of success for a sensitive spirit as a writer when his ideals are altogether outside the domain of popular taste is treated in *Pierre*. And in *The Confidence Man*, Melville's picture of Americans as ignorant, ego-starved, money-hungry, credulous, and altogether at the mercy of cunning, ingratiating dissimulators and pelican-like ego-flatterers, is as chilling

as it is appalling. *The Confidence Man* is a unique achievement in a special kind of nihilism whose real appraisal has
yet to be made.

EMERSON'S ATTACKS ON SOCIETY

So much in this brief survey for the dark American Romantic. What of the light? Ralph Waldo Emerson, the originator of
the phrase, was all his life a sayer of *No*. The whole of his career, from the time of his resignation of his ministerial pulpit
in the Unitarian Church over the rite of the Holy Communion—which he believed to be barbarous—was devoted to at-
tacking materialism, opportunism, complacency, parochi-
alism, and conformity. America might have been a lofty land,
but it was now peopled by little men. Politics was too often a
machinery for perpetuating prejudice and cant and for working injustice and inhumanity. When the United States passed
the Fugitive Slave Law in 1851, Emerson in cold fury damned
it in the pages of his *Journals* and wrote, "I will not obey it,
by God." He condemned the infamous war of aggression
against Mexico. As for society,

> Society everywhere is in conspiracy against the manhood of
> every one of its members. Society is a joint-stock company, in
> which the members agree, for the better securing of his bread
> to each shareholder, to surrender the liberty and culture of
> the eater.

Society was vitiated by a "vulgar prosperity which retro-
grades ever to barbarism."

> 'Tis the day of the chattel:
> Web to weave and corn to grind.
> Things are in the saddle
> And ride mankind.

Yet everywhere men put their faith in society and boasted of
progress. "All men plume themselves on the improvement of
society, and no man improves," observed Emerson sardon-
ically. No more than Hawthorne could he declare a new social pattern good if the hearts of those to live within it were
still unregenerate. So indefatigably, imaginatively . . . , in poetry and in prose, he appealed to the consciences of American young men and women, urging them to take a stand
against wrong belief, wrong habit, wrong life.

> 'Tis our perdition to be safe
> When for the truth we ought to die.

"Nothing is at last sacred but the integrity of your own

mind." But Emerson's attacks came from the fact that he loved his country and its principles, of which he was intensely aware. If its citizens lived in such a way that the profit motive was not their passively adopted leading motive and the divine could enter their lives, "a nation of men" would *"for the first time* exist." And his ideal of America would be achieved—a land of "beautiful faces, warm hearts, wise discourse, and heroic acts."

THOREAU AND WHITMAN

Henry David Thoreau held convictions similar to those of Emerson, but, as Emerson himself confessed, he obeyed them far more in the acts of his daily life. He attacked the same weaknesses of his native land and mercilessly derided progress as "improved means to an unimproved end." He not only fulminated against the government for its perpetuation of iniquitous slavery and its heinous waging of war against Mexico; he refused to pay his poll tax which would enable it to do so. His writing, which, he admitted, was his effort to educate his fellow Americans to a knowledge of right living, was more intense than Emerson's—sharper, pithier, more trenchant in its phrasing. At times it was truculent. "The mass of men lead lives of quiet desperation," he declared in *Walden;* they "begin digging their graves as soon as they are born." Old people, having never lived, were repositories of ignorance only, not of wisdom. In thirty years Thoreau had never heard a word of valuable advice from a single one. In America, as in Europe, clothing fashion called the tune. "The head monkey at Paris puts on a traveler's cap, and all the monkeys in America do the same." As for the individual in his conformity to convention and decorum,

> The American has dwindled into an Odd Fellow—one who may be known by the development of his organ of gregariousness, and a manifest lack of intellect and cheerful self-reliance . . . who, in short, ventures to live only by the aid of the Mutual Insurance Company, which has promised to bury him decently.

To place Walt Whitman in the roster of Romantic sayers of *No* may seem queer, since we all remember Whitman as a great, perhaps the greatest, affirmer of America. Yet just as it is . . . true that Whitman's love of life was inextricably linked to his preoccupation with death, so also we can say that his faith in America's future grew out of his recognition of her defects and miscarriages of the past. . . . The many references to the defeated and slain, to the unjustly treated and exploited, to convicts, prostitutes, drunks, and slaves, in, say, Whitman's jubilant *Song of Myself,* is only to point out instances of universal human weakness or perfidy found in any work which aims to treat human experience honestly and comprehensively. Still the fact is that they are evidences that things were not all well in America in 1855 and that Whitman knew it. In such a prose piece as the preface to the second edition of *Leaves of Grass* or *Democratic Vistas,* a work whose aim is precisely to look ahead into the future, we find Whitman's candid assessment of the state of the new nation and an account of the many things he said *No* to. He did not flinch from "truths none the less terrible."

> I say that our New World democracy, however great a success in uplifting the masses out of their sloughs, in materialistic development, products, and in a certain highly-deceptive superficial popular intellectuality, is, so far, an almost complete failure in its social aspects, and in really grand religious, moral, literary, and esthetic results.

A UNIQUE CHARACTERISTIC OF AMERICAN ROMANTICISM

Now it is not this quality of *No*-saying which makes American Romantics romantic. But it *is* this quality more than any other which makes them different from other Romantics. And it certainly is one of the qualities which make them great. . . .

But this quality is not peculiar to American writers of the Romantic period only. It characterizes great authors throughout the history of American literature. As [literary critic] Roy Harvey Pearce has observed, "the power of American poetry from the beginning was derived from the poet's inability, or refusal, at some depth of consciousness wholly to accept his culture's system of values." Without any wrenching of meaning here the word "poet" can be changed to "author."

In this respect American literature is unique. French literature exhibits no such preoccupation. Nor does English in spite of the passionate identification from time to time of English writers with England, as in Milton's fervent "millennarianism" in his pamphleteering of the 1640s, or as in Wordsworth's sonnets: "We English are sprung of earth's first blood. We have titles manifold." Germany had no nationhood, nor did Italy, until after the mid-19th century, which means that irrespective of a profound feeling for the soil or for the *people* (Das Volk) as in the case of the German 19th century lyric poets, or even for native land (as in the case of Machiavelli in the 16th century, in whose nostrils the occupying barbarians from the north were a stench), the literature of neither country was similar to that of America. But it is the continuous and, one is tempted to say, systematic way it addresses itself with intense consciousness to the nation's practice, as well as to the profession of certain ideals, which distinguishes American literature from all others.

America as a nation was founded rather late on the world scene. And it is all-important that its birth occurred not in the 17th century but in the 18th, during the Enlightenment. The sense of a world community then being what it was, and political idealism being widespread, the founders of the new nation, as Thomas Jefferson admitted, were obliged to explain to the rest of the world why they were doing what they were doing and what they expected to gain by it. The date of the founding of the new nation is so recent—only 200 years ago—that American writers have grown up with the principles stamped on their minds. And many of them have been, so to speak, watchdogs guarding those principles proudly and jealously, with an instinct always to assess the extent to which they have been fulfilled. This is as much as to say that American literature is a literature of idealistic dissent—the American Romantics were dissenters from popular values for the sake of an ideal (although the ideal in the case of Poe was, as we have seen, something utterly unrelated to the fulfillment of national destiny). Though generally overlooked, this is an important fact. As Robert Penn Warren, one of our most distinguished poets, has observed,

> There has been a lack of a spirituality [in America], if you want to call it that. . . . You have a whole series of the major writers who are violently critical of America. . . . What they say is not being told to the student. . . . And what the implications are of our American literature. It's an extremely critical literature, critical of America and constantly rebuking America and trying to remake it.

CHAPTER 2

Transcendentalism

American
Romanticism

Transcendentalism Was a Religious and Intellectual Movement

Mark Richard Barna

In the following selection, freelance writer Mark Richard Barna contends that Transcendentalism was a revolt against traditional Christian beliefs about God, as well as a divergence from philosopher John Locke's assertion that knowledge is acquired through the senses. Instead, Transcendentalists believed in the "eternal ONE"—the notion that within each person resides a universal soul that provides flashes of intuition, considered by Transcendentalists to be the most profound form of knowledge.

In 1836, a group of New Englanders began to gather regularly to discuss new spiritual ideas. Over the years the group would include Amos Bronson Alcott, a Neoplatonist and a talker of apostolic brilliance; Rev. Theodore Parker, a scholar of German and a staunch critic of orthodoxy; and Margaret Fuller, erudite, intelligent, with the women's movement of the latter half of the century gestating in her head. There were also Rev. Orestes Brownson, a keen thinker and controversial Christian writer; Rev. George Ripley, a born critic of literature, passionate in his disgust for the form and ritual of the church; and Rev. William Ellery Channing, who in 1819 became the unofficial spokesperson for American Unitarianism. Poets like Jones Very and Christopher Cranch frequented the discussions too, along with a recent Harvard graduate still looking for his place in life named Henry David Thoreau.

At the center of the group was a man who usually remained quiet, listening attentively, and occasionally moving the discussion along on its lofty strain with a percipient comment. It was not that he was the leader; it was enough

Excerpted from Mark Richard Barna, "The Transcendental Impulse." This article first appeared in *Gnosis Magazine*, Spring 1995. Reprinted with permission.

that he was there. He was Ralph Waldo Emerson.

The group shared the belief that the theory propounded by John Locke in the seventeenth century—that knowledge can be apprehended only through the senses—was false. Moreover all of them had recently become interested in the response to Locke's philosophy made by the German Idealists in the eighteenth century. From this foundation, the conversations would take flight and sometimes soar to reveal, according to Emerson, "glimpses of the Universe, hints of power native to the soul, far-darting lights and shadows of an Andes landscape, such as we can hardly attain in lone meditation."

With such influential men and women meeting regularly for conversation, the Boston newspapers began reporting when and where the meetings would take place, while referring to the participants as the "Transcendentalists." The name stuck.

From 1840 through 1844 the Transcendentalists had their own magazine, *The Dial,* which they used as a vehicle to express their ideas to the public. This period might well be considered the high-water mark of Transcendentalism as a bona fide, cohesive religious movement.

Transcendentalism was an admixture of Unitarianism, Puritanism, German Idealism, Platonism, Neoplatonism, and Asian religions. Throughout its history it remained endemic to the vicinity of Boston and was primarily embraced by visionaries, intellectuals, and disaffected Unitarian ministers. Scholars have called it the "ultimate Protestantism," "Calvinism modified by the assumption of the innate goodness of man," "Pyrrhonism," and "literary religion"; the public called it "The Walden Pond Society." It had no church, no ritual, no list of members, and no statements of belief; all it had was regular meetings for conversation and a magazine with a circulation of less than 1000.

In this viewpoint I will attempt to make sense of a religious movement that never really made sense of itself, yet continues to influence late twentieth-century spiritual thought. I will do this by examining the writings and lives of the two men who most completely and profoundly embodied its essence: Emerson and Thoreau. In their writings certain ideas consistently reappear. It is these that form the "statements of belief" (that is, if there ever *were* any) of American Transcendentalism.

THE WORLD IN GOD

Though Emerson renounced many Christian tenets after re-signing his Unitarian pulpit in 1832 to become a "scholar-at-large," he never quite renounced them all. The traditional Christian belief in the subordination of matter to soul or spirit always remained the central assumption of his philosophy. His readings of Plato and the Neoplatonists reinforced this belief. When he later began reading Eastern texts, he found these ideas again and began incorporating their metaphors and terminology (such as *Brahma, Paramatman,* and *maia*) into his writings.

Emerson's book *Nature* (1836) is in some ways a manifesto for the movement. The Transcendentalists read it with relish. Henry Seidel Canby, a biographer of Thoreau, says it is one of two books that most influenced Thoreau's thinking (the other being *The Bhagavad Gita*).

In this passage from *Nature,* Emerson uses the word "Reason" (a Kantian term he derived from Coleridge) to indicate a world beyond the senses.

> When the eye of Reason opens, to outline and surface are at once added, grace and expression. These proceed from imagination and affection, and abate somewhat of the angular distinctness of objects. If the Reason be stimulated to more earnest vision, outlines and surfaces become transparent, and are no longer seen; causes and spirits are seen through them. The best, the happiest moments of life, are these delicious awakenings of the higher powers, and the reverential withdrawing of nature before its God.

Emerson looks upon the world as "one vast picture, which God paints on the instant eternity, for the contemplation of the soul."

There is a subtlety here that is easily missed. Emerson is not seeing pantheistically—God in the world—but transparently—"the world in God." But this does not satisfy him, for it "leaves God out of me." Emerson suggests that the mind is also part of the world, for "many truths arise to us out of the recesses of consciousness." God therefore "does not build up nature around us, but puts it forth through us, as the life of the tree puts forth new branches and leaves through the pores of the old." In his 1842 lecture "The Transcendentalist," he elucidates this point.

> [The Transcendentalist's] experience inclines him to behold the procession of facts you call the world, as flowing perpetually outward from an invisible, unsounded centre in him-

self, centre alike of him and of them, and necessitating him to regard all things as having a subjective or relative existence, relative to that aforesaid Unknown Centre of him.

Such a philosophy makes possible this bold statement: "His thought—that is the Universe." In this light we see that the Transcendentalists' reverence for nature is not just for its beauty but for its insights into the nature of God.

In his 1872 essay "Poetry and Imagination," Emerson takes this belief in a phenomenal world to its logical extreme, replete with Eastern terminology. "Youth, age, property, conditions, events, persons—self, even—are successive *maias* (deceptions) through which Vishnu mocks and instructs the soul."

This concept was the core of Transcendentalism.

The Eternal ONE

Emerson was raised to believe that God was Other, aloof from the world. Divine laws were separate from natural laws (coming together only when it was God's will) and man was separate from God. Emerson found an alternative to this thinking in the writings of the third-century Neoplatonist Plotinus, who believed that everything was contained within the "all-encompassing One." In Emerson's 1841 essay "The Over-Soul," his debt to Plotinus is evident: "Within man is the soul of the whole; the wise silence; the universal beauty, to which every part and particle is equally related; the eternal ONE."

In addition, the Platonic idea of "reminiscences" resurfaces, though in a slightly modified form. Plato believed that our soul contains all knowledge; and according to an explanation by Thomas Taylor, Emerson's favorite translator of Plato, "whatever knowledge she [the soul] acquires in the present life, is in reality nothing more than a recovery of what she once possessed." This fits logically into the schematics of Transcendentalism. If everything is within "the eternal ONE," then the human mind is connected to all ages—past, present, and future. Robert D. Richardson Jr., author of a recent biography of Thoreau, explains this concept: "The human mind has always been the same. It has neither progressed nor declined from age to age. Chronology, therefore, is not important in history. All ages are equal; the world exists for the writer today just as it did for Homer. The present is as high as the past, and vice versa."

In *Walden* (1854) Thoreau writes:

> The oldest Egyptian or Hindoo philosopher raised a corner of
> the veil from the statue of the divinity; and still the trembling
> robe remains raised, and I gaze upon as fresh a glory as he
> did since it was I in him that was then so bold, and it is he in
> me that now reviews the vision. No dust has settled on that
> robe; no time has elapsed since that divinity was revealed.

SIMPLICITY, SIMPLICITY, SIMPLICITY

Thoreau's Walden experiment is the seminal example of
Transcendentalism in practice. Why would a bright Harvard
graduate repudiate the professions and live in a one-room
cabin in the woods? He had one spoon and one cup, he borrowed an ax to cut down some trees, he drank and bathed at
Walden Pond, and when offered a welcome mat to lay before
his door, he refused, for he felt the chore of shaking loose its
dirt to be too great. "Simplicity, simplicity, simplicity!" says
Thoreau. "Let your affairs be as two or three, and not as a
hundred or a thousand; instead of a million count half a
dozen, and keep your accounts on your thumb-nail."

In the days of the Transcendentalists, Manifest Destiny
was the ringing cry. Virgin forests and prairies waited to be
conquered, factories to be built, fortunes to be made. Here
was a young nation feeling its oats in the Promised Land;
and here was Thoreau with the prescience to see the error.

> Men labor under a mistake. The better part of the man is soon
> plowed into the soil for compost. By a seeming fate, com-
> monly called necessity, they are employed, as it says in an old
> book, laying up treasures which moth and rust will corrupt
> and thieves break through and steal. It is a fool's life, as they
> will find when they get to the end of it, if not before.

Despite the biblical reference, Thoreau's antipathy for
worldly riches was not Christian (at least in a conventional
sense) but Transcendentalist. It was not to win a place in
heaven, nor was it to deny oneself in order to placate a
wrathful God; instead it was to transcend the pull of the apparent world for "the eternal ONE."

Thoreau is advocating spirituality, not simplemindedness.
There are savages who live simply in the outward sense, as
Thoreau had read of the Hawaiian Islanders. In their case,
he felt, outward simplicity was accompanied by "idleness"
and "its attendant vices" and was no better than the complex
life of society. Nor is Thoreau advocating that society be
abandoned for the woods. After all, his poet friend, Ellery

Channing (son of William), had tried the primitive life on the Illinois prairie and found no spiritual advantage in it. No, the change must be inward. "Be a Columbus to whole new continents and worlds within you," Thoreau advises, "opening new channels, not of trade, but of thought."

ORIGINS OF TRANSCENDENTALISM

Unitarianism was a product of the Enlightenment and as such was highly rationalistic. It disavowed the orthodox doctrines of the Trinity, the atonement, and the divinity of Jesus. Instead it upheld the veracity of conscience, the brotherhood of man, and the ability of persons to achieve religious awakening by their own efforts. This liberal version of Christianity became popular with many Bostonians, and the Harvard Divinity School in Cambridge soon became the chief seminary for the Unitarian Church. But the younger ministers were becoming increasingly dissatisfied with what Emerson was later to call its "pale negations."

In 1819 William Ellery Channing attempted to rectify this situation with a sermon that would become the central document of American Unitarianism. In it he pleaded with his audience to search God's word for themselves and to allow their divine inspiration to flow into poetry and religious fervor. Not only was Channing revitalizing a decaying Unitarianism, but he was also laying the groundwork for Transcendentalism.

The term "transcendental" was taken from the German philosopher Immanuel Kant. In the *Critique of Pure Reason,* Kant, in answer to Locke, contended that the senses *cannot* provide full knowledge of the world. Indeed we do not even know whether our senses are perceiving the world aright. Furthermore, we cannot know God, the self, or the cosmos by the senses, for all is governed by an unknowable "transcendental ego." Emerson's knowledge of Kant was taken from Coleridge and Carlyle, and consequently Kant's philosophy is somewhat refracted in Emerson. Whereas Kant argued that God (or indeed anything) is ultimately unknowable, Emerson says that Kant's "imperative forms, which do not come from experience," can be known intuitively. "Hence, whatever belongs to the class of intuitive thought is popularly called at the present day *Transcendental.*"

Intuition, Emerson believed, should have precedence over the intellect. This was the belief of the post-Kantian German

Idealists, whom Emerson read with a discerning eye. Since Concord had once been Puritan, the impress of Puritanism remained deep and lasting even upon the minds of the town's most forward thinkers. Thus Transcendentalism, by the nature of its environment, could not embrace the Germans' sallies into atheistic radicalism and moral ambiguity. As a result, a philosophy developed that, while lauding ecstasy and intuition, also found room for ethics, discipline, and grace....

INTUITIVE THOUGHT

In "The Transcendentalist," Emerson tells of

> a certain brief experience which surprised me in the highway or in the market, in some place, at some time—whether in the body or out of the body, God knoweth—and made me aware that I had played the fool with fools all this time. . . . Well, in the space of an hour probably, I was let down from this height; I was at my old tricks, the selfish member of a selfish society.

"Yet there is a depth in those brief moments," he writes in "The Over-Soul," "which constrains us to ascribe more reality to them than to all other experiences." We have all had these moments. They seem to occur randomly, unaided by special fortune or the machinations of the intellect. It is a moment of perfection, of grace, of a glimpse beyond the finite. It is an oasis in the common desert of our life. "Our virtue comes in moments; our vice is habitual."

"Intuitive thought" is the concept most identified with the Transcendentalists. It is also the most misunderstood. To some it has sounded like the 1960s slogan "if it feels good, do it," generating accusations of antinomianism and irresponsibility. The Transcendentalists seem to be advocating anarchy.

But beneath this arabesque lay the steel foundation of moral law. Puritan and Asian asceticism, Unitarian conscience, and Greek discipline conspired to ground any licentious flights.

To read the "Higher Laws" chapter in *Walden* is like returning to the days of Puritan zeal. "Chastity is the flowering of man," writes Thoreau. "Man flows at once to God when the channel of purity is open. "He then warns of the dangers when we "eat [meat], or drink [tea, coffee, alcohol], or cohabit, or sleep sensually." It matters not which is indulged in; for Thoreau they are all the same. "They are but one appetite, and we only need to see a person do any one of these things to know how great a sensualist he is." At the close of "Higher Laws," Thoreau tells the story of John Farmer (a symbol of Everyman), who, after a hard day of labor, listens to a voice within.

> —Why do you stay here and live this mean moiling life, when a glorious existence is possible for you? Those same stars twinkle over other fields than these.—But how to come out of this condition and actually migrate thither? All he could think of was to practise some new austerity, to let his mind descend into his body and redeem it, and treat himself with ever increasing respect.

The appeal to ethics, conscience, and asceticism are everywhere in Transcendentalist writings, but none is more important than the call for humility. For it is humility that allows the proper hierarchy to be established. "Let us take our bloated nothingness out of the path of the divine circuits," writes Emerson. "Let us lie low in the Lord's power."

The Transcendentalist Fall is not set in the dim past; it is in the present. It occurs the moment our will supersedes a Higher Will, or maybe better said, the moment we think we *have* a will to supersede. Nothing has fallen. The blank is in our own eye, says Emerson. We need only awaken. By living intuitively and righteously, a renewal, a self-transcendence, can occur—without the baggage of eternal redemption.

This was how the Transcendentalists made their way into, and then through, Christian orthodoxy. . . .

TRUST THYSELF

There is a common thread running through these beliefs. The concept of the One suggests that the multifarious things we see and experience are mere appearances; this suggests that abstractions like time are as well. Without time we are left only the present. Here is where eternal truths manifest in the form of intuition and inspiration. Our will interferes and separates us from the One; simplicity, ethics, grace—and self-reliance—bring us back. And since we are One—one mind—we have every right to trust our thoughts. "To believe your own thought," writes Emerson in "Self-Reliance," "to believe that what is true for you in your private heart is true for all men—that is genius. Speak your latent conviction, and it shall be the universal sense." Why defer to another when all are of one mind? Why look to past oracles? Within you is the wisdom of the ages. "Trust thyself."

Transcendentalism Is a Philosophy of Optimism

Paul F. Boller Jr.

Paul F. Boller Jr. is the author of several books on American thought and United States history. In the following selection, excerpted from American Transcendentalism, 1830–1860: An Intellectual Inquiry, *Boller asserts that a defining characteristic of Transcendentalism is its tireless optimism. The Transcendentalists' view of mankind as infinitely good led to accusations that the philosophy was unrealistic and superficial, and that it ignored the injustices, suffering, and evil in the world.*

British Romantic writer Thomas Carlyle is said to have taken Ralph Waldo Emerson once on a harrowing trip through the London slums and then exclaimed: "Well, do you believe in a devil now?" To Carlyle, Emerson's confident cheerfulness about the world was a curious spectacle; and his wife, Jane, was frankly put off by it. Charles Eliot Norton . . . was similarly perplexed; he regarded Emerson's optimism as a kind of bigotry and said that if Emerson went to hell by mistake he would probably either deny its existence or pronounce it the abode of good and the realm of order. "He has not allowed himself to doubt the supremacy of the best in the moral order," wrote Norton impatiently. "He is never weary of declaring the superiority of assertion and faith over negation!"

Norton's was a common complaint in Emerson's own day and after. Hawthorne, whose dark novels repelled Emerson, called Emerson a "mystic, stretching his hand out of cloudland, in vain search for something real," and he satirized Transcendentalism in his story "The Celestial Railroad." Herman Melville also had satirical things to say about Transcen-

Excerpted from Paul F. Boller Jr., *American Transcendentalism, 1830–1860: An Intellectual Inquiry* (New York: Putnam, 1974). Reprinted with permission from the author.

dentalism in *The Confidence Man;* and in both *Moby Dick* (1851) and *Pierre* (1852) he took sharp issue with some of its basic affirmations. [Literary critic] John Morley rebuked Emerson for overlooking "the vileness, the cruelty, the utter despicableness to which humanity may be moulded"; [writer] Henry James, Jr., thought Emerson's "ripe unconsciousness of evil" gave him a narrowly limited view of the world; [literary critic] George Santayana said that Emersonian Transcendentalism ignored injustice, suffering, and impotence in the world; and William Butler Yeats regarded it as superficial because it lacked a vision of evil. "I love your *Dial*," Carlyle once told Emerson,

> and yet it is with a kind of shudder. You seem to be in danger of dividing yourself from the Fact of this present universe, in which alone, ugly as it is, can I find any anchorage, and soaring away after Ideas, Beliefs, Revelations, and suchlike—into perilous altitudes, as I think. . . . Alas, it is so easy to screw one's self up into high and ever higher altitudes of Transcendentalism, and see nothing under one but the everlasting snows of Himmalayeh . . . easy . . . but where does it lead? Well, I do believe, for one thing, a man has no right to say to his own generation, turning quite away from it: "Be damned!" It is the whole Past and the whole Future, this same cotton-spinning, dollar-hunting, canting and shrieking, very wretched generation of ours. Come back into it, I tell you.

Edgar Allan Poe, for his part, said he would like to hang the editor of *The Dial*.

Charges of Transcendental insensitivity to the dark side of life could be multiplied almost indefinitely, but they all tended to be overstated. The Transcendentalists were not precisely complacent optimists; they found much to rail against in their own day and age. Emerson has been called a "militant Pollyanna," yet he was not unaware of the sadness of things. He once referred to the "ghastly reality of things" and decided, when he was thirty-two, that after the age of thirty a person wakes up sad most mornings the rest of his life. There was an austere—even bleak—note in Transcendentalism, for all its joyous assertions; and Europeans like Friedrich Nietzsche, Charles Baudelaire, and André Gide, scarcely noted for their facile optimism, read Emerson's essays with profound respect and admiration. Still, there is no doubt that the Transcendentalists regarded their faith as an invigorating one and that they preferred (especially in the salad days of the movement) affirmation to negation. When Emerson and Margaret Fuller got out the first number of *The Dial* in July, 1840, they announced in a letter from the editors to the readers, their clear intention of elevating people to a higher platform of aspiration, making life less desultory, and removing melancholy from the landscape. "We wish," they said, explaining the name *Dial,* "it may resemble that instrument in its celebrated happiness, that of measuring no hours but those of sunshine. Let it be one cheerful rational voice amidst the din of mourners and polemics." During its four years of existence, *The Dial* succeeded in faithfully (too faithfully, Carlyle thought) recording the sunshine. In addition to publishing poetry, literary criticism, book reviews, and discussions of music, painting, sculpture, and religion, it also presented such essays as "The Divine Presence in Nature and the Soul," "The Art of Life," "Ideals of Everyday Life," "What Is Beauty?" and "Christ's Idea of Society." In its last issue, April, 1844, Emerson's essay "The Tragic" showed how intellect and moral sense could "ravish us into a region" where "clouds of sorrow cannot arise." And the last sentence in the final number, concluding a short notice of a book on human nature, announced that *"the highest good for man consists in a conscious increase and progression in Being, or assimilation to God."*

TRANSCENDENTAL HOPES

All the Transcendentalists, even the prickly Thoreau, believed deeply in an inevitable *"increase and progression of Being."* "Surely joy is the condition of life," wrote Thoreau in *The Dial.* "I love to live," he wrote elsewhere.

> I love reform better than its modes. There is no history of how bad became better. I believe something, and there is nothing else but that. I know that I am. I know that another is who knows more than I, who takes an interest in me, whose creature, and yet whose kindred, in one sense, am I. I know that the enterprise is worthy. I know that things work well. I have heard no bad news.

As he grew older, Thoreau did become increasingly aware of evil in nature, in the form of decay and death, and at times it gave him pause; to the end, however, he continued to assert "the glory of the universe" and its "steady onward progress." His friend A. Bronson Alcott was even more affirmative about life; his was probably the serenest of all the Transcendental temperaments. "His attitude," said Thoreau admiringly, "is one of greater faith and expectation than that of any man I know." For Alcott, evil was no problem; he minimized its reality. "Evil no *nature* hath," ran one of his imperturbable *Orphic Sayings;* "the loss of good is that which gives Sin its livelihood." What is the bad, he once asked, "but lapse from the good,—the good blindfolded?" He also transcendentalized evil by saying that it was a kind of condiment which gave relish to good or was like the dark background in a picture which made beauty and goodness stand out all the more vividly by its contrast. [Transcendentalist scholar] Theodore Parker wrestled with the problem of evil more earnestly than Alcott, but he also concluded that there was more gladness than sadness in the world and that evil was a transient phenomenon in God's creation. Pain and suffering, he said, served as warnings and deterrents to save man from worse mishaps; they also usually came from ignorance and failure of adaptation and were thus indispensable stimuli to efforts to increase our knowledge and understanding of the universe. All in all, then, there was "a perfect system of optimism in the world" for Parker; evil was resolved in a higher good, and there was endless progress toward perfection going on in the universe. Margaret Fuller, for her part, fully shared her friends' optimism. "Evil," she said, echoing Alcott, "is abstraction; Good is accomplishment." She knew frustration and disappointment in abundance, yet she never gave up her faith in "the divine soul of this visible creation, which cannot err or will not sleep, which cannot permit evil to be permanent or its aim of beauty to be eventually frustrated in the smallest particular." She once reduced her creed to two articles of belief: "I believe in Eternal Progression. I believe in a God, a Beauty and Perfection to which I am to strive all my life for assimilation."

PROGRESS AS THE LAW OF HUMANITY

If the Transcendentalists believed in the preponderance of good in the universe, they also had high hopes for the future of humanity. "The work of the ages goes on," affirmed George Ripley, even after the failure of [the utopian community] Brook Farm;

> man advances nearer to the freedom which is his birthright; the temporary evils, that are incidental to all transitions from an old order of things to a better, pass away, and are forgotten; the self-sustaining, self-recovering power of liberty, in-

sures the health of the social body; and . . . the serene spirit
of humanity unfolds new strength and beauty in the elastic
atmosphere of liberty, until its presence is acknowledged
universally as benign.

As a social activist, Orestes Brownson, like Ripley, thought
that humanity had made tremendous progress in past ages
and was destined to move steadily forward. "We must neither
feel nor act as if all progress was ended," he wrote, "and mankind had attained all the perfection of which he is capable.
There is to be a progress through all the future, as there has
been one through all the past; but the future progress must

TRANSCENDENTALISM IN THE WORDS OF EMERSON

The first thing we have to say respecting what are called
new views here in New England, at the present time, is, that
they are not new, but the very oldest of thoughts cast into the
mould of these new times. The light is always identical in its
composition, but it falls on a great variety of objects, and by so
falling is first revealed to us, not in its own form, for it is form-
less, but in theirs; in like manner, thought only appears in the
objects it classifies. What is popularly called Transcendentalism
among us, is Idealism; Idealism as it appears in 1842. As
thinkers, mankind have ever divided into two sects, Materialists
and Idealists; the first class founding on experience, the second
on consciousness; the first class beginning to think from the data
of the senses, the second class perceive that the senses are not final, and say, the senses give us representations of things, but
what are the things themselves, they cannot tell. The materialist
insists on facts, on history, on the force of circumstances, and the
animal wants of man; the idealist on the power of Thought and
of Will, on inspiration, on miracle, on individual culture. These
two modes of thinking are both natural, but the idealist contends
that his way of thinking is in higher nature. He concedes all that
the other affirms, admits the impressions of sense, admits their
coherency, their use and beauty, and then asks the materialist
for his grounds of assurance that things are as his senses represent them. But I, he says, affirm facts not affected by the illusions
of sense, facts which are of the same nature as the faculty which
reports them, and not liable to doubt; facts which in their first
appearance to us assume a native superiority to material facts,
degrading these into a language by which the first are to be spoken; facts which it only needs a retirement from the senses to
discern. Every materialist will be an idealist; but an idealist can
never go backward to be a materialist. . . .

always be elaborated in the present." Frederick Henry Hedge was another Transcendentalist who believed that society was always moving onward. "Notwithstanding the perpetual flux and reflux which appears on the surface of things," he explained in the article "Progress of Society" (1834), "there has been an undercurrent of improvement coextensive with the whole course of time. There never was an age in which some element of humanity was not making progress." William H. Channing also believed that the end of existence was growth and that progress was the vital law of humanity. He proclaimed his faith in a manifesto appearing in the *Western Mes-*

In the order of thought, the materialist takes his departure from the external world, and esteems a man as one product of that. The idealist takes his departure from his consciousness, and reckons the world an appearance. The materialist respects sensible masses, Society, Government, social art, and luxury, every establishment, every mass, whether majority of numbers, or extent of space, or amount of objects, every social action. The idealist has another measure, which is metaphysical, namely, the *rank* which things themselves take in his consciousness; not at all, the size or appearance. Mind is the only reality, of which men and all other natures are better or worse reflectors. Nature, literature, history, are only subjective phenomena. Although in his action overpowered by the laws of action, and so, warmly cooperating with men, even preferring them to himself, yet when he speaks scientifically, or after the order of thought, he is constrained to degrade persons into representatives of truths. He does not respect labor, or the products of labor, namely, property, otherwise than as a manifold symbol, illustrating with wonderful fidelity of details the laws of being; he does not respect government, except as far as it reiterates the law of his mind; nor the church; nor charities; nor arts, for themselves; but hears, as at a vast distance, what they say, as if his consciousness would speak to him through a pantomimic scene. His thought,—that is the Universe. His experience inclines him to behold the procession of facts you call the world, as flowing perpetually outward from an invisible, unsounded centre in himself, centre alike of him and of them, and necessitating him to regard all things as having a subjective or relative existence, relative to that aforesaid Unknown Centre of him.

Ralph Waldo Emerson, "The Transcendentalist," a lecture read at the Masonic Temple, Boston, January 1842.

senger when he took over as editor in May, 1840:

> Man's restlessness is a sign of his grand destiny. Even misdi-
> rected energies reveal his greatness. The whole discipline of
> providence is a proof of God's interest and regard. . . . God is
> training man to the art of virtue. . . . [We] see a progress in the
> past history of our race; we feel that a mighty power of good
> is stirring now in society; we believe in the coming of the
> kingdom of God.

For [New England scholar] J.F. Clarke, the progress of the
human race was fixed "by laws as immutable as the nature
of God.". . .

In their teleological view of creation, Transcendentalists
like Emerson were profoundly optimistic. Their vision may
have been austere, but it was hopeful, not tragic, in the large.
Like Hegel (and like Marx, too), they believed in cosmic
progress; they thought the world was unfolding according to
an immanent, necessary, and beneficent plan. It is a view
which still has a powerful appeal for many people and nations in the contemporary world.

The Role of Nature in Transcendentalism

Lawrence Buell

In this excerpt from *Literary Transcendentalism: Style and Vision in the American Renaissance,* literary critic Lawrence Buell describes the role of nature in Transcendentalist thought. Although Transcendentalists were lovers of nature, he writes, they were far more interested in the pursuit of philosophical truths. In their writings, nature often appears as a metaphor that illustrates their beliefs about life.

Nature as a literary pursuit was an acquired taste for the Transcendentalists, sometimes never acquired at all. The majority of Transcendentalist ministers, for example, were content to celebrate "nature" and "cosmic unity" as splendid abstractions and perhaps dash off a few poems in their spare time on the "tender flush of vernal dawn" or the sublimity of Niagara Falls. The prestige of *Walden* has taught us to associate Transcendentalism with a "return to nature," but in fact Thoreau was a less typical figure in this respect than Margaret Fuller, who "delighted in short country rambles" but was too nearsighted, unhealthy, and citified to convey much more than a tourist's enthusiasm for what she saw. She did write some interesting verse and prose-poetry on natural subjects, and some patches of good descriptive prose; but on the whole nature plays a minor role in her writing, and in her literary criticism she has almost nothing to say on the subject. Her love of nature was strong, but it did not much affect her literary personality.

Most of her fellow Transcendentalists also have more to say about Genius, Beauty, and Truth than about Nature. Even those who wrote most about nature arrived at their subject only after a preliminary period of meditation on religion, the conduct of life, and other matters similarly ab-

Excerpted from Lawrence Buell, *Literary Transcendentalism: Style and Vision in the American Renaissance.* Ithaca: Cornell University Press, 1973. Reprinted with permission from the author. (Footnotes in the original have been omitted in this reprint.)

struse. Although James Russell Lowell was pig-headed in refusing to concede Thoreau much knowledge of nature, he was right that Thoreau had relatively little at the start of his career. Indeed, almost all the Transcendentalists, perhaps even Thoreau, were closer to being humanists than naturalists. At bottom they were more interested in man than nature, more interested in thought than observation. "What is Nature unless there is an eventful human life passing within her?" Thoreau asks. "A single good man, at one with God," says Theodore Parker, "makes the morning and evening sun seem little and very low." The deliberate appraisals of nature made by all the Transcendentalists fall between these two degrees of qualification. The central preoccupation of the movement was the relationship between self and God; compared to this, nature was of secondary importance.

But though the Transcendentalists were primarily children of the Puritans rather than children of nature, their reverence for the natural creation surpassed their ancestors', and with reason. To begin with, nature was no longer a threat or obstacle to survival. Whereas for the Puritans the "howling wilderness" was a hostile force, for the Transcendentalists it could serve as a sentimentally attractive image of the vigor and spontaneity lacking in their more comfortable existence. Beyond this, their distrust of historical Christianity made them attach an unusually high theoretical value to nature as evidence and analogue of man's relation to God. This attitude, in turn, was reinforced by the romanticist cult of nature, particularly the vision of an organic universe, and by the nationalist cliché of America as nature's nation, which seemed to make romanticist ideology all the more relevant to their situation. As a result, nature tended to become a crucial touchstone in matters of religion, as when Emerson condemned the doctrine of miracles as monstrous because "it is not one with the blowing clover and the falling rain." Some Transcendentalists thought this too radical, but the general drift of the movement was from the rational supernaturalism of the Unitarians to natural religion to the religion of nature.

THE ROLE OF NATURE IN ART

In their aesthetics, likewise, the Transcendentalists relied heavily upon the analogy of nature whenever they went further than simple celebrations of inspiration and genius and undertook to discuss style and form. As scholarship has conclusively and repeatedly established, they accepted the romantic-expressivist principle of organic form, believing that the work of art, rather than adopt an arbitrary pattern, should take shape like an organism according to the nature of the thing expressed. The *locus classicus* of this motif in Transcendentalist thought is Emerson's declaration in "The Poet" that "it is not metres, but a metre-making argument that makes a poem,—a thought so passionate and alive that like the spirit of a plant or an animal it has an architecture of its own, and adorns nature with a new thing.". . .

The basis of Transcendentalist thinking as to the role of nature in art is the idea of a metaphysical correspondence between nature and spirit, as expressed chiefly by Emerson. Man and the physical universe, Emerson says, are parallel creations of the same divine spirit; therefore natural and moral law are the same and everything in nature, rightly seen, has spiritual significance for man. The universe is thus a vast network of symbols—a Bible or revelation purer than any written scripture—which it is the chief task of the poet to study, master, and articulate. He above all others is qualified for this task because, unlike the theologian and the scientist, who attempt to reduce the meaning of nature to a rationalistic system, the poet follows the method of nature herself: he is guided by inspiration rather than logic, and expresses his thoughts in the form of images, in the same way that nature expresses spirit. A good literary work is therefore not an artificial construct, but a "second nature," growing out of the poet's mind as naturally as the leaf of a tree.

CHAPTER 3

Nature in American Romanticism

Nature and the American Consciousness

Joshua Johns

The following selection was taken from *Purple Mountain Majesty: Sublime Nature in the U.S. Capitol,* a website that explores American perceptions of nature. Joshua Johns, the developer of the site, describes how American Romanticism challenged the predominant view of nature as a savage wilderness and an impediment to civilization.

When Frederick Jackson Turner announced in 1893 that "the American character did not spring full-blown from the Mayflower," but that "it came out of the forests and gained new strength each time it touched a frontier," his speech punctuated nearly three centuries of examinations into the American wilderness. From Jamestown and Plymouth Plantation to the Louisiana Purchase of 1803 and the subsequent expedition of Lewis and Clark, to Turner's "Frontier Thesis" at the Columbian Exposition of 1893, the geography and ecology of the American continent was the center of debate among Americans. Two primary views of the wilderness were contested: the wilderness either contained savagery and temptation which threatened the authority of the community or it represented a new Garden which could flourish with the proper cultivation by the European settlers. Although these contrasting views of the wilderness shared the goal of establishing a civilization by removing the obstacles presented by the natural environment, the state of wilderness that originally characterized the young nation eventually became the source of national pride and identity for America.

In an essay entitled "The Cultural Significance of the American Wilderness," Roderick Nash notes that early settlers in the New World were not Americans at all, but trans-

Excerpted from Joshua Johns, "A Brief History of Nature and the American Consciousness," from *Purple Mountain Majesty: Sublime Nature in the U.S. Capitol,* available at http://xroads.virginia.edu/~CAP/NATURE/cap2.html. Reprinted by permission of the author.

planted Europeans who regarded the land as a spiritual and physical void which had to be conquered and civilized in the name of Christianity and progress. Because it was an unknown entity with bizarre animals, unusual topography, and strange indigenous inhabitants, the wilderness represented a place where community and consensus would be put in peril by the total absence of European law, religion, and civilization. Early New England literature, art, and folklore presents the wilderness as the place where reason succumbs to passion and the devil can seduce and corrupt even the holiest in the community. In other early colonies, particularly Pennsylvania and Virginia, the wilderness represented the Garden—a place to be tamed and cleared for the establishment of a human community. In this outlook, however, the land supplied the raw materials for building a society, and nature was to be used, not feared. Despite the different outlooks, the goal was the same: to destroy the savage wilderness and make it bloom with European civilization. . . .

During the Lewis and Clark expedition in the Jeffersonian era, the primary goal of wilderness investigation was to take inventory of the garden and complete a taxonomy of the American continent. Jefferson's interest in taxonomy was supported in Pennsylvania by the Philosophical Society of Benjamin Franklin, a group of scientists that included anthropologist Charles Wilson Peale, botanist Benjamin Rush, and chemist/physicist Joseph Priestley. Jefferson and the men of this society often compared notes and shared the results of individual experiments to assess and quantify the land and its contents. Although these men displayed a genuine curiosity about their environment, they were eager to discover what resources of economic value lay in the land for their use in building a civilized society. Northern strides toward industry and technology led by Franklin, and Southern emphasis on the idealized agrarian society of gentlemen's farms espoused by Jefferson, shared a desire to tame and contain the wilderness by imposing upon it a constructed landscape of human civility and divine order. The wilderness exploration of Jefferson's time suggested that America's success as a nation was tied to the cultivation of the wilderness. America could have a rural character, but not a wild one. To achieve our "manifest destiny," Americans had to create a pastoral middle landscape of rolling hills and prosperous farms. . . .

CHANGING PERCEPTIONS OF NATURE

By the middle of the nineteenth century, cities and towns were blooming across the east and the midwest, and people were looking for ways to ease the toil of cultivating and harvesting the American garden. Robert Fulton's steamboat, first launched in 1807, and the development of Eastern railways represented the first intrusions of what Leo Marx would call "the machine in the garden." With these early stirrings of the industrial age to come, Americans began to examine their relationship to the land around them. The birth of the Hudson River school of American painting, signalled by George Innes's *The Lackawanna Valley*, married wilderness with civilization in harmonious depictions of pastoral rural towns gleaming with the prosperity brought to them by the broad-based economy of both agriculture and technology. Authors such as Washington Irving and James Fennimore Cooper turned to the still-wild woods of upstate New York as settings for their stories and inspiration for their frontier-minded characters. Neither group was particularly critical of their changing relationship to nature, but the advent of technology now meant that civilization had gained considerable advantage in the continuing struggle between the garden and the wilderness.

The more penetrating of these examinations into the changing landscape emerged during the 1850's and 1860's in the writings of Ralph Waldo Emerson and Henry David Thoreau during the early era of the American Renaissance, which was influenced in part by British Romanticism. Nature was once again a subject for American art and letters, but the perceptions of it had shifted to reflect the new American concern with the changes in the landscape. Rather than presenting nature as an obstacle to the establishment of a civilization, American authors and painters alike upheld nature as the source of the animating spirit behind the American character. . . .

The Romantics approached the subject [of nature] from a different perspective. Romanticism set up opposition to the Neoclassic insistence on order and hierarchy by championing individual freedom through man's relationship to nature. The Romantics believed that nature was the inherent possessor of abstract qualities such as truth, beauty, independence and democracy. In the natural world, people could reclaim or at least approximate the lost innocence of their origins—both individual and national. The image of America as a garden could apply to the Romantic perspective of nature, but the gridwork of civilization had to be stripped from the landscape. The original state of American wilderness—as well as areas of the country yet undeveloped—gave America a valid claim to a possession now desirable in European thought. Wild nature thus became a source of national pride as the root of character traits for a unique national identity. This embrace of wilderness released at last a true native creativity in the American mind. No longer bound by classical notions of art and literature in Europe, many American

AMERICAN ROMANTICISM AND ORGANIC STYLE

Both Ralph Waldo Emerson and Henry David Thoreau would have objected energetically to having their work evaluated by its approximation to other art instead of to nature. . . . Thoreau laid down the proposition that 'there are two classes of men called poets; the one cultivates life, the other art,' and left no doubt about which he wanted to be. Emerson said, 'Ask the fact for the form,' thereby enunciating his conviction that art must be based organically on nature. He believed that the tendency of an artificially refined society is always 'to detach the beautiful from the useful,' to lose sight of the functional in trivial and effeminate ornamentation. In affirming that the duty of the artist is continually to renew elemental experience, Emerson also subscribed to Samuel Taylor Coleridge's conception of how the artist creates his forms. Coleridge's key-passage on the organic principle, which arose from his discussion of William Shakespeare, sums up the central idea that is to be developed in this chapter:

> No work of true genius dares want its appropriate form, neither indeed is there any danger of this. As it must not, so genius can not, be lawless; for it is even this that constitutes it genius—the power of acting creatively under laws of its own origination. . . . The form is mechanic, when on any given material we impress a pre-determined form, not necessarily arising out of the properties of the material;—as when to a mass of wet clay we give whatever shape we wish it to retain when hardened. The organic form, on the other hand, is innate; it shapes, as it develops, itself from within, and the fulness of its development is one and the same with the perfection of its outward form. Such as the life is, such is the form. Nature, the prime genial artist, inexhaustible in diverse powers, is equally inexhaustible in forms.

F.O. Matthiessen, *American Renaissance: Art and Expression in the Age of Emerson and Whitman*, 1941.

artists and authors disregarded European traditions and began to explore the natural world of America for its possibilities of new subject matter. . . .

Representations of sublime nature expressed for Americans the roots of their national character. Not only did the Edenic portrayal of America give it the status of a promised land, but also turned it into a country where true equality— among the European setters at least—could prevail, and freedom could exist in as pure a form as ever existed in Europe. Peggy Wayburn of the University of California states that "the wilderness of the continent made obsolete and alien the old ideas of rank, caste, and inherited aristocracy . . . common man could become uncommon man.". . . As Turner would argue in his thesis, the obstacles presented by the wilderness fostered the beloved American traits of independence, ingenuity, pragmatism, and resourcefulness, and the existence of a rolling frontier line which was constantly redrawn and redefined both geographically and politically as each stage of western expansion continually reaffirmed national faith in democracy and equality.

American Romantics View Nature as a Metaphor for the Self

Bernard Rosenthal

Bernard Rosenthal has edited a number of books of literary criticism and is the author of *Salem Story: Rereading the Witch Trials* and *City of Nature: Journeys to Nature in the Age of American Romanticism*, from which the following selection was excerpted. He maintains that American Romantic writers saw nature as a representation of the self.

The common denominator of American Romanticism, probably of all Romanticism, may be found in the attempt to create a private world free from the constraints of time and history. Romantic writers want to reject predestination, mechanism, or any theory of history that denies individual preeminence in the shaping of events. Accordingly, in articulating a theory of history, Ralph Waldo Emerson found an understandable appeal in a rhetorical question Napoleon asked: "What is history . . . but a fable agreed upon?" In the same essay, "History" (1841), Emerson further concludes that "All history becomes subjective; in other words there is properly no history, only biography." If history as an absolute process could be turned to private biography, malleable in the mind of the poet, the individual would be free to enter a world of infinite possibility—the location of Romanticism.

But the Romantic writer is also compelled to acknowledge the constraints imposed by linear history, as Emerson indeed does in "History":

> But along with the civil and metaphysical history of man, another history goes daily forward—that of the external world—in which he is not less strictly implicated. He is the compend of time; he is also the correlative of nature. His power consists in

Excerpted from Bernard Rosenthal, *City of Nature: Journeys to Nature in the Age of American Romanticism* (Newark: University of Delaware Press). ©1980 by Associated University Presses, Inc. Reprinted with permission from Associated University Presses.

the multitude of his affinities, in the fact that his life is intertwined with the whole chain of organic and inorganic being.

Out of the vast quantity of critical study on American Romanticism, agreement has emerged on at least one point: American Romantics experienced a conflict between themselves and the culture within which they lived, between the myth they sought to create and the historical world in which they were "implicated." Whether, as A.N. Kaul argues, they sought to resolve this through creating an ideal of community, or whether, as Richard Poirier affirms, they looked for "a world elsewhere," modern scholarship has correctly acknowledged the fundamental tension between the Romantics and their "external world." But the relationship between the two has been only partially understood, since comprehensive attempts at examining such American concepts as "nature," the "garden," or the "city" have generally presupposed that these terms had meanings common to the Romantics and to the other people who inhabited the country in which they shaped their art. If such a supposition is false, then the definitions need to be clarified, and the premises underlying the "tension" between the artist and society require reexamination.

DIFFERING PERCEPTIONS OF NATURE

American Romantics, being "implicated" in linear history, took their language, their metaphors, their tropes, from the "external world." Primarily, they shaped into private meanings American categories of thought centering on images of nature. Stated another way, Americans of the day generally held a set of myths about nature, and from these public myths the Romantics reconstructed a vocabulary to express radically different private myths. Regardless of how odd their definitions of nature may appear upon close examination, the people who inhabited Emerson's "external world" had reasonably common understandings of nature's meanings. These understandings differed profoundly from Romantic perceptions of nature, even though Romantic writers appropriated national images of nature to their own ends.

The Americans of Emerson's "external world" perceived nature primarily as participating in a teleological process shaped in part by man and culminating in civilization. Nature in its most important and pervasive metaphorical use connoted the values of civilization and often implied civilization itself. In its purest form, nature took the shape of urban America, and the journey to nature became the journey to the city. In a world that held to this sensibility, Emerson and his contemporaries came of age. Because of their implication in an "external world," the American Romantics defined their interior journeys in a language that also brought them from nature to the city. If Leo Marx has drawn different conclusions from observing this pattern of their journeys, he has nevertheless accurately noted that "our American fables" lead heroes through "a raw wilderness. . .back toward the city." But toward what city, and through what nature do our fables lead us? The answer to this depends on whether the journey occurs in historic America or in private myth, a distinction Henry David Thoreau suggests in his essay "Walking":

> I walk out into *a* [italics added] nature such as the old prophets and poets, Menu, Moses, Homer, Chaucer walked in. You may name it America, but it is not America; neither Americus Vespucius, nor Columbus, nor the rest were the discoverers of it. There is a truer account of it in mythology than in any history of America, so called, that I have seen.

The truest history of nature, Thoreau tells us, cannot be found in any history of America. Nor is nature one phenomenon, as his indefinite article indicates. Thoreau walks to "a" nature, discovered earlier by poets, explorers of man's interior world. In the region of romantic myth, Thoreau can walk the same ground they did. But it is a different ground from that upon which the people of his day walk. Put another way, Thoreau has not simply posed history against myth; he has confronted his myth with his culture's myth. Americans had constructed a story about nature, which Thoreau rejected, though he would use the frame of that story in describing his own interior journey. This story of nature in early nineteenth-century America, whether told in novels, travel narratives, or political orations, recounted the transformation of nature into its purest form, civilization. It was not the only story of the time, but it was the most pervasive, and it found its greatest teller in James Fenimore Cooper. . . .

The counterpart to the myth Cooper essentially endorsed exists in the myth of nature as spiritual place, the region comparable to where Thoreau walks in the paths of Menu, Moses, Homer, and Chaucer. One does not need trees or lakes here, although one may certainly use them, as one uses whales. Similarly, one may use America, as Walt Whitman does in "Passage to India," as he passes through America's historical triumph over the West to embark on a "Passage to more than India," to a mythic sphere that leaves the linear history of America behind. It is an interior journey to a private place, one that ultimately takes the poet as far from an American location as Thoreau takes the reader in "Walking," where he finds the "truer account" of "nature" in "mythology" rather than in America. All our classic writers of the Romantic period, except for Cooper, explored mythic regions analogous to those found by Whitman and Thoreau. . . .

All writers, of course, do not fit neatly into one category or the other, nor is the canon of any given author ever wholly devoted to a single view. Yet, broadly speaking, a distinction may be made between those primarily concerned with the "external world" and those who sought to find a different order of understanding in a new religious myth generally called Romanticism.

It is no understatement to say that Romanticism has many connotations, but without entering into the debate Arthur O. Lovejoy precipitated by his moderate insistence that the term requires definition, I want to cite Northrop Frye's *A Study of English Romanticism* to establish my own use of the term. According to Professor Frye, the

> Middle Ages itself, like all ages, had its own anti-mimetic tendencies, which it expressed in such forms as the romance, where the knight turns away from society and rides off into a forest or other "threshold symbol" of a dream world. In Romanticism this romance form revives, so significantly as to give its name to the whole movement, but in Romanticism the poet himself is the hero of the quest, and his turning away from society is to be connected with . . . the demoting of the conception of man as primarily a social being living in cities. He turns away to seek a nature who reveals herself only to the individual.

Additionally, "the great Romantic theme is the attaining of an apocalyptic vision by a fallen but potentially regenerate mind."

Literary historians reasonably enough associate this regeneration with an "Adamic myth," but there must be no misunderstanding about the state of Adam in this myth as it took shape in America. Adam was fallen and not innocent. The successful romantic quests, such as those found in *Nature*, *Walden*, or "Song of Myself," all posit the fallen figure seeking to *restore* a diminished or lost spirituality. Conversely, the quests of Herman Melville, Nathaniel Hawthorne, and Edgar Allan Poe generally reveal probings at regeneration accompanied by a failure to achieve it, at least if one reads these writers as governed by Melville's "blackness." But whether finding success or failure in the quest for regeneration, all of them—Emerson, Thoreau, Whitman, Melville, Hawthorne, Poe—explore "the great Romantic theme.". . .

THE END OF THE ROMANTIC JOURNEY

At some point in the nineteenth century, and historians may debate exactly when, the American journey into nature ended. The political frontiers had been conquered, and Western man, as Whitman affirms in "Passage to India," had circumnavigated the globe. If the American West was not a totally idyllic place, it nevertheless essentially redeemed the pledge of material prosperity nature had held. Political and economic problems remained, but the American journey to nature had been relatively successful. The romantic journey was also largely over in the sense that new methods of literary exploration engaged the attention of leading writers such as Henry Adams, Stephen Crane, Henry James, and Mark Twain, although inquiries into the meaning of being remained fundamental to their writing. What had generally changed was the pattern of metaphor. Whether coincidental or not, the *romantic* trope of a journey to nature in search of salvation ended at about the time that American[s] fully possessed the promised land.

Except for Melville's *Clarel* and *Billy Budd,* the last richly poetic nineteenth-century exploration of what had already become an old dream appeared in Whitman's "Passage to India." The poem, dated 1871, explores again the romantic myth that by then bordered on nostalgia. Since Melville's later writings offer only bleak possibilities, "Passage to India" remains as the final great nineteenth-century example of the romantic dream that in the "Passage to more than India," as Whitman phrased it in his poem, a truly new metaphysical and redemptive frontier could emerge. Melville, as early as 1849, had insisted in *Mardi* that such quests led to places other than those Whitman imagined in his poem. Yet both writers probed the "mythology" of Thoreau's "Walking." In the polarities of human possibility outside of geographical America, one thrusting toward hope and the other toward a hopeless endurance, "Passage to India" and *Mardi* exemplify the similar meanings to be found in so many journeys to nature taken by Romantic writers.

Both narratives recognize that, in Whitman's words, "the shores of America," or of this world, are too confining, that "this separate Nature," as Whitman calls the tangible world, is "so unnatural." One must shed the temporal, as the poet does in seizing command of his soul and launching "out on trackless seas" in search of "unknown shores." Whitman is "bound where mariner has not yet dared to go," and is ready to "risk the ship, ourselves and all." Whitman's "trackless seas" may be equated with Melville's "endless sea" and "chartless" voyage across "untracked" waters. Whitman, who will "steer for the deep waters only," is like Melville's hero Taji, who grasps possession of his own soul, seizes the helm of his ship with "eternity . . . in his eye," and daringly plunges forth. Before the final moment of these two journeys, where the heroes leave all temporal things behind and move toward the mystical "unknown shores," each author has first taken the reader through a linear history. Both writers have invoked Europe and America; each has found them "so unnatural"; each has sought to redefine the self in a region beyond the world of physical things, regardless of different expectations. In "Passage to India" an old Walt Whitman still follows the promise that

> Nature and Man shall be disjoin'd and diffused no more,
> The true Son of God [the poet] shall absolutely fuse them.

We recognize in the vision its kinship to Emerson's prophecy of 1836 that the "problem of restoring to the world original and eternal beauty is solved by the redemption of the soul." This world defined by Emerson as one that "lacks unity, and lies broken and in heaps" will be put together again. Melville, in sending his hero across the "endless sea," makes no such promise. But the quests are similar in their intentions, and they have little to do with Cooper's American journeys.

THE DREAM OF THE ROMANTICS

In 1855 when Whitman announced himself to the world in *Leaves of Grass* he did so with the implicit promise that the words of Emerson would be validated. In "Passage to India" he was still uttering the promise, as if by a kind of Shelleyan incantation he could make it happen. Emerson was saying little at this time about putting the world back together again. By 1871, for a generation of writers, the restless, long-ing dream that art might in some way make coherent the in-coherent world was for the most part over.

Their dream had generally implied that if science ren-dered chaotic the old divine order, perhaps the world might yet be held together by something called *nature*. Not the na-ture that Whitman thought of as "unnatural," but something else: the peculiar amalgam of all tangible things seen through the religious eye that transformed them into an idea whereby nature would transcend its physical qualities. To this region of nature beyond India, heroes of a literary era embarked on their inner journeys to Walden, or to Ishmael's sea, or to the "place" in *Nature* where Emerson's "poet" found a way of knowing that would transform old beliefs into a new myth. Such explorations are neither peculiar to America nor to the nineteenth century. But the American writers who created such journeys drew heavily from an im-age fundamental to those living in their "external world." The discovery of nature became the discovery of civilization, or the self, as the Romantics modified the pattern.

The American journey was successful; it was a rewarding passage whereby a nation transformed the wilderness into something approximating the urban dream it held for na-ture. The romantic journey had a different outcome. Cast of-ten in the lyric language of success, as in *Walden, Nature,* or "Passage to India," the inner quest for what these works of art prophesied was generally unfulfilled, and nature rarely kept the promise it had seemed to make. Indeed, nature of-ten evoked a threatening myth, often suggested that all the seas might not be those of God. On the other side of Walden Pond one might find "A Winter Walk," where Thoreau thinly covers with snow the death and decay he implicitly defines as something other than nature:

> The wonderful purity of nature at this season is a most pleas-ing fact. Every decayed stump and moss-grown stone and rail, and the dead leaves of autumn, are concealed by a clean napkin of snow.

This world of death and decay lurked just underneath the "clean napkin" of nature. When the "napkin" was probed, however, when the world was explored, it often appeared in its ambiguity of whiteness. "Think what a mean and wretched place this world is," writes the creator of *Walden* in another book, "that half the time we have to light a lamp that

we may see to live in it. This is half our life. Who would undertake the enterprise if it were all? And, pray, what more
has day to offer? A lamp that burns more clear, a purer oil,
say winter-strained, that so we may pursue our idleness
with less obstruction. Bribed with a little sunlight and a few
prismatic tints, we bless our Maker, and stave off his wrath
with hymns."

"Who would undertake the enterprise if it were all?" That
was the crucial question, and the Romantics hoped that it
would not be "all." Somewhere there might be something
else; not in the realm of America's nature, but in the private
vision of the questing individual. This is by no means to say
that all the Romantics spent their entire lives monomania-
cally searching for God or some equivalent. Obviously, they
found other satisfactions. But when nature served as the
metaphor for the regenerative quest, when artists sought
their location in the universe, the passage took them to a region away from geographical America, away from any geographical place, to a mythic nature where they could escape
from an "unnatural" plight. And they dared the search, even
though the "seas of God" proclaimed by Whitman in 1871
had too often proved to be, in Melville's words, the "realm of
shades." They searched in the region of Thoreau's "mythology" rather than in the America from which they took much
of the imagery that described their separate journey.

Emerson's and Thoreau's Understanding of Nature

Ann Woodlief

Ann Woodlief is a professor of English at Virginia
Commonwealth University in Richmond, Virginia.
She has published a number of scholarly articles
on Transcendentalism. In the following selection,
excerpted from a paper presented to the Virginia
Humanities Conference, Woodlief compares Ralph
Waldo Emerson's and Henry David Thoreau's per-
ceptions of nature. She contends that both writers,
Thoreau in particular, were prophets of the environ-
mentalist movement.

Ralph Waldo Emerson's greatest gift was lessons in seeing in
and through nature and extracting symbolic meaning, yet
his own intimate encounters with the nature around him
were relatively rare and indirect, with few concrete traces in
his writings except as occasional metaphors. He wanted his
revelations from nature to be abstract and come by surprise,
as did the famed mystical encounter at the beginning of his
book *Nature:* "Crossing a bare common, in snow puddles, at
twilight, under a clouded sky, without having in my
thoughts any occurrence of special good fortune, I have enjoyed a perfect exhilaration. I am glad to the brink of fear."
In such an experience, even the self is absorbed by a greater
power: "I become a transparent eye-ball; I am nothing; I see
all; the currents of the Universal Being circulate through
me." The metaphor may be unfortunate, but not his faith
that a single person could perceive unspeakable meanings
through experiencing nature, even if only indirectly. Such
possibilities impelled Henry David Thoreau and countless
others since to mine the details and processes of nature that

Excerpted from Ann Woodlief's paper, "Emerson and Thoreau as American Prophets
of Eco-Wisdom," for the Virginia Humanities Conference, 1990. Reprinted with permission from the author.

Emerson had generalized, looking for embedded revelations and sharing in nature's "ecstasy."

In *Nature* Emerson takes an unabashedly anthropocentric view, seeing nature as a great and holy teacher of the self-reliant man who will look beyond its uses as mere commodity and see it as infused with spirit, with a wonder known to few adults. Nature's purpose was clear to Emerson: "All the parts incessantly work into each other's hands for the profit of man" and "the endless circulations of divine charity nourish man." Nature's beauty and accompanying tonic of delight come through "the plastic power of the human eye" which lets us appreciate natural things "in and for themselves" yet it also finds "correspondences" which translate the landscape into human meaning; "Particular natural facts are symbols of particular spiritual facts." Nature provides the alert man with fresh images and metaphors for language, giving the man with the discipline to devote himself to its study ultimate power: "One after another, his victorious thought comes up with and reduces all things, until all the world becomes, at last, only a realized will,—the double of the man." Power and self-revelation come only when one can see each particle of nature as a microcosm, which "faithfully renders the likeness of the world."

Yet there are moments, particularly in the last half of *Nature* and some lectures, when Emerson modifies his exuberant anthropocentrism. Though he never put humans on the same moral level as animals or trees, for example, he does see them all linked as the expression of Spirit, which may only be described in terms of natural laws and unified fluid processes. The self is both humbled and empowered in its cosmic perspective. By knowing the harmony of nature's laws, the poet or philosopher can see through it, making "the refractory world . . . ductile and flexible," yet he also recognizes that Nature is "inviolable" and "serene," not "subjected to human will." Any reforming or changing of nature, then, must come from "redemption of the human soul." The true naturalist must "satisfy all the demands of the spirit. Love is as much its demand, as perception"; only then can he obey the Orphic poet's injunction to "Build, therefore, your own world.". . .

THOREAU'S UNDERSTANDING OF NATURE

Emerson was evidently more comfortable with the idea of anthropocentrism, as was Thoreau at moments in *Walden* and his early journal. However, Thoreau went on to explore the more recalcitrant facets of Nature's otherness, that wildness, as he called it, which had little or no correspondence with human needs or desires. His understanding of self-reliance enabled him to appreciate the resisting independence and integrity of nature. Only recently have literary critics learned to value the work which truly challenges both its readers and the anthropocentric stance, especially his later journal. Here Thoreau rejected Emerson's more transcendental rhapsodizing about perceiving nature as symbol of the human mind for a rigorous exploration of his natural world which was constantly—and productively—frustrated in its search for personal and human meaning in an almost alien world of nature. As [professor and literary critic] Sharon Cameron demonstrates, readers who assume connections of meaning between nature and man are troubled by his efforts in the journal to speak in nature's voice, putting human concerns on the margin of "nature's infinite self-referentiality." That effort to speak about what is, by Thoreau's definition, humanly unspeakable, may be doomed, but that is part of its transcendental reach as well as his unique literary accomplishment.

Thoreau has become the prophet of wilderness for modern environmentalists who have adopted as motto his assertion that "in Wildness is the preservation of the World." Although he did advocate that each town should set aside extensive acreage in its natural state as "a common possession forever for instruction and recreation," and he traveled through the Maine wilderness, he was more comfortable in a semi-domesticated Concord than in true wilderness, such as the untamed ocean depths which had Herman Melville questioning God. His limit for handling wildness seems to have been reached on Mt. Katahdin, where nature's unresponsive materiality made him feel his humanity and spirit slipping away. Though he recognized nature's separateness, he continued to try to "redeem" it, to give it some human order and meaning with his observations. Paradoxically, he thought nature needs man to make it significant yet nature must also remain essentially separate from humans. . . .

What were the practical consequences of his belief in nature's separate independence, aside from the torrent of observations and unanswered questions which fill his later journals? Paradoxically, it expanded rather than curtailed his own sense of humanity. He felt one must behave as morally toward nature as toward men, and considered the wasteful cutting of the forests, for example, to be inhumane. In 1855 he wrote about his decision not to hit the chestnut tree with a stone to bring down nuts, saying "It is not innocent, it is not just, so to maltreat the tree that feeds us." Yet his motive was not just self-serving. . . . He suggests that he would be murdering a "sentient being—with a duller sense than my own, but yet a distant relation" and advises that "if you would learn the secrets of Nature, you must practice more humanity than others." He ends sharply by asking, "Behold a man cutting down a tree to come at the fruit! What is the moral of such an act?"

THOREAU AS A CONSERVATIONIST

Economy was also a crucial aspect of his response to nature, especially at Walden. Although he uses the word in *Walden* as a quasi- or anti-business metaphor, it is also an early ecological term. Thoreau copied long extracts from Linnaeus' work on "The Oeconomy of Nature," adopting his phrase to describe interdependent relationships within nature. His effort to live in harmony with nature at Walden required the literal economy of using as few resources as necessary. Not only did he find time and freedom to read, write, and think by reducing his consumption to a minimum, but he could live with more integrity in nature by adapting to its seasons, not interfering with its processes, and honoring its own "oeconomy." He built his cabin by recycling boards, cutting only the wood necessary to frame it, and heated his stone fireplace with driftwood. He grew beans without fertilizer, pesticides, or weed killer, ate little meat, owned few clothes, bathed in the pond, and walked everywhere he wanted to go. Reducing life to its simplest terms left him free to observe and appreciate the natural economy around him. His economic self-sufficiency may not transfer easily to an urbanized people enslaved to petroleum, but he had the right idea—to think, before you consume, of the consequences to your mental and spiritual health which depends so much on an intimate and moral, even "humane," connection with nature.

There are other transcendental strains in Thoreau which ring true today. As we try to rescue vanishing species, he lamented the loss of "nobler animals," regretting that his ancestors have "torn out many of the first leaves and grandest passages" of the poem of primitive nature, thwarting his desire "to know an entire heaven and an entire earth." He was fascinated with the Indian, whose "intercourse with Nature is at least such as admits of the greatest independence of each," envying his "rare and peculiar society with nature"— one denied even to himself. Though an inventive person himself, he distrusted the technology of the railroad and machines, wondering about the American obsession with speed. Science, he feared, is "inhuman. Things seen with a microscope begin to be insignificant. . . . With our prying instruments we disturb the balance and harmony of nature." On the most transcendental level, though, he turned to nature for a beauty and harmony, even a civilized humanity, which he often found lacking in ordinary life, cherishing nature's "eternal health" and "perfect confidence." Yet even in these moments he noted that he "had seen into paradisaic regions" where he had "hardly a foothold."

Feeling an intimate part of nature yet also aware of its separate integrity, Thoreau found there the very roots of his vitality, his art, and his religion. Both he and Emerson pointed the way for us, who live in a more diminished and often polluted nature, to discard our false sense of dominion and superiority and discover our proper ethical and spiritual place in nature.

Differing Perceptions of Nature in American and European Romanticism

Tony Tanner

In the subsequent selection, excerpted from *Scenes of Nature, Signs of Men,* Tony Tanner argues that American and European Romantic writers differed in the way they experienced, perceived, and wrote about nature. Tanner is a Fellow at King's College in Cambridge, England, and the author of several books on American and British authors of the nineteenth and twentieth centuries.

One of the formative experiences of early American writers was of a sense of space, of vast unpeopled solitudes such as no European Romantic could have imagined. As the hero of Chateaubriand's *René* says to his American auditors: 'Europeans constantly in a turmoil are forced to build their own solitudes.' The reverse was true for the American Romantic. Solitude was all but imposed on him. Nothing seemed easier for him than to take a few steps to find himself confronting and caught up in those measureless oceans of space where Walt Whitman found his soul both surrounded and detached. This gravitation towards empty space is a constant in American literature, even if it appears only in glimpses, as for instance when the narrator of *The Sacred Fount* turns away from the crowded house of Newmarch and staring up at the sky finds the night air 'a sudden corrective to the grossness of our lustres and the thickness of our medium'; or when the narrator of *The Last Tycoon* says 'It's startling to you sometimes—just air, unobstructed, uncomplicated air.' Charles Olson is justified in starting his book on Herman Melville (*Call me Ishmael*) with the emphatic announcement: 'I take

Excerpted from Tony Tanner, *Scenes of Nature, Signs of Men.* © Cambridge University Press 1987. Reprinted with the permission of Cambridge University Press.

SPACE to be the central fact to man born in America, from Folsom cave to now. I spell it large because it comes large here. Large, and without mercy.' But like those spiders who came under [18th century religious scholar] Jonathan Edwards's formidable scrutiny, the American artist, once he found himself at sea in space, had to do something to maintain himself, and one instinctive response was to expand into the surrounding space. William Cullen Bryant writes of 'The Prairies': 'I behold them from the first, / And my heart swells, while the dilated sight / Takes in the encircling vastness'; Whitman claims 'I chant the chant of dilation'; Ralph Waldo Emerson records how 'the heart refuses to be imprisoned; in its first and narrowest pulses it already tends outward with a vast force and to immense and innumerable expansions . . . there is no outside, no inclosing wall, no circumference to us'. Emerson's eye, and his mind after it, was continually drawn to the remotest horizons; the only true encirclement to a man obsessed with circles was earth's vanishing point, the very perimeter of the visible world where sight lost itself in space. When he writes about 'The Poet' and his attraction to narcotics of all kinds Emerson says: 'These are auxiliaries to the centrifugal tendency of a man, to his passage out into free space, and they help him to escape the custody of that body in which he is pent up, and of that jail-yard of individual relations in which he is enclosed.' Near the end of *Walden* Henry David Thoreau has some marvellous lines about the 'ethereal flight' of a hawk which sported alone 'in the fields of air'. 'It appeared to have no companion in the universe . . . and to need none but the morning and the ether with which it played.' Thoreau ends the book, appropriately enough, with the parable of the bug which hatches out in an old table and breaks free into 'beautiful and winged life', and Whitman at the end of *Song of Myself* literally feels himself diffused back into the elements: 'I depart as air . . .' In these three seminal American Romantics we find a similar 'centrifugal tendency'; a dilation of self, which can become an abandoning of self, into the surrounding vastness. . . .

Those American writers we associate with the New England Renaissance (and many subsequently) most typically felt themselves to be swimming in space; not, certainly, tied fast into any society, nor really attached very firmly to the vast natural environment. In many ways this state was cherished and preferred; to sport in fields of air could be the ultimate ecstasy. On the other hand there was the danger of, as it were, vanishing or diffusing altogether. The emergent strategy, variously developed by different writers, was to spin out a web which could hold them in place, which would occupy the space around them, and from which they could look out into the world. But even when they scrutinized their environment with extreme care, and took over many of its details to weave into their webs of art, they were seldom in any genuine communion with nature. European Romantics, on the other hand, do seem to have enjoyed moments of reciprocal relationship with nature and could speak truly of what they 'half perceive and half create'. With William Wordsworth they could consider 'man and nature as essentially adapted to each other'. In discovering nature they were at the same time discovering themselves; in internalizing what was around them they were at the same time externalizing what was within, as Samuel Taylor Coleridge often described. 'The forms / Of Nature have a passion in themselves / That intermingles with those works of man / To which she summons him.' That is Wordsworth, and it is just that sort of fruitful *intermingling* of Nature's and Man's creative potencies that is absent from American Romantic writing, which tends, rather, to testify that Nature holds off from man's approaches. Nature is indeed seen, seen with intense clarity through the intervening air, but it leaves precisely that intervening space to be filled by the writer's own filament. That marriage between subject and object, mind and nature, which is an abiding Romantic dream, is seldom consummated in the work of the American Romantics. When Emerson speaks of 'the cool disengaged air of natural objects' he is pointing to a perceptual experience which makes for important differences in American Romanticism.

EMERSON'S VISION OF NATURE

Of course it would be an unacceptable simplification of Emerson's strangely fluid writing to fix on any one of his descriptions of nature as his definitive attitude. But in his first famous essay on 'Nature' we find a conception of nature markedly different from any to be found in any comparable European documents. Above all it is the fluidity, the insubstantiality, the transparency of nature which is stressed. Emerson may sound like Wordsworth when he talks of 'that wonderful congruity which subsists between man and the world'—so much was a stock Romantic piety, or hope. But what a strange congruity Emerson's is. To the poet, he says, 'the refractory world is ductile and flexible'. When a poetic mind contemplates nature, matter is 'dissolved by a thought'. The Transcendentalist, says Emerson (and Transcendentalism was pertinently described as 'that outbreak of Romanticism on Puritan ground' by [New England scholar] James Elliot Cabot) has only to ask certain questions 'to find his solid universe growing dim and impalpable'. The 'poet turns the world to glass'; when he looks at nature he sees 'the flowing or the Metamorphosis'. 'The Universe is fluid and volatile': 'this surface on which we now stand is not fixed, but sliding'. If there is any 'fixture or stability' in all this sliding, dissolving, melting world, it is 'in the soul'. 'We are not built like a ship to be tossed, but like a house to stand', says Emerson. Since his Nature is distinctly watery, and the 'ethereal tides' seem at times almost to inundate him as he opens himself to them, we may wonder what will be the origin of this stable house of self which can stand firm in the flowing flux of Existence.

Although Emerson is sometimes very specific about individual facts and perceptions, the nature he refers to has no autonomy and very little local identity. It is a mental fabrication. We look in vain for the specificity of all those place-names which are so common in European Romanticism, whether it is Tintern Abbey or Mont Blanc or 'Lines Composed while Climbing the Left Ascent of Brockley Coome, Somersetshire, May 1795' (Coleridge). Emerson says that America's 'ample geography dazzles the imagination' and a dazzled imagination may respond in unusual ways. His own response, more often than not, is to treat nature as a flimsy, flowing tissue of appearances. He is concerned either to see through it, or withdraw from it. It is indeed a source of emblems, but he tends only to assert this emblematical quality. Perhaps the difference between an emblem and a metaphor is that an emblem is a sign existing at a definite remove from what it signifies and composed of different material; while a metaphor merges the sign and the thing signified. For Emerson Nature was more a matter of emblems than metaphors; it provided no final resting place, no home, for the mind. Here, perhaps, we can detect vestiges of the old Puritan suspicion of matter as fallen, flawed, and misleading—despite Emerson's programmatic optimism about the essential benevolence of all creation. However it is, Emerson's Nature lacks the substantiality, the local external reality, to be found in many European Romantic writers. In Emerson Nature may be a symbol for the mind, or a manifestation of the invisible Over-Soul. What it tends not to be is its own solid self. Children, said Emerson, 'believe in the external world'. When we grow older we realize that it 'appears only'. Perhaps Emerson found no more dramatic phrase for his concept of Nature than when he suggested it might be 'the apocalypse of the mind'.

What Emerson has done is to interpose his version of a ductile, transparent, fluid, apparitional nature between himself and the hard, opaque, refractory (and dazzling) otherness of the real American landscape. This way he makes Nature amenable to himself and his purposes. It is notable how often he talks of playing with Nature as if it were a collection of baubles and toys. The genius, he writes in his journal, 'can upheave and balance and toss every object in Nature for his metaphor'; we must be like Shakespeare, he says, who 'tosses the creation like a bauble from hand to hand'. Anything less tossable from hand to hand, less bauble-like, than the American landscape in the mid-nineteenth century would be hard to think of. But Emerson is swimming in air; and this Nature, this flowing stream of soft transparent playthings, is the web he has created to keep himself afloat. By contrast Wordsworth's or John Keats's poetic Nature is, if not the apocalypse of reality, at least its consecration. . . .

THE WILD LANDSCAPE OF AMERICA

Another point is worth making, which is put clearly in the poem written by Bryant for the [American] painter Thomas Cole as the latter was about to leave for Europe. First Bryant reminds Cole of the wonderful wild and savage landscapes which he has painted (and which indeed he loved), then he warns him of what he will see in Europe:

> Fair scenes shall greet thee where thou goest—fair,
> But different—everywhere the trace of men,
> Paths, homes, graves, ruins, from the lowest glen
> To where life shrinks from the fierce Alpine air—
> Gaze on them, till the tears shall dim thy sight.
> But keep that earlier, wilder image bright.

In Europe, 'everywhere the trace of men': in America, 'that wilder image'. Bryant himself is clearly appreciative of both, but he more particularly wants to retain 'that wilder image'

which the as-yet uncivilized landscape of America can provide. The wildness of this landscape was felt to have values
and provide spiritual nourishment not available in Europe.
'We need the tonic of wildness', says Thoreau, while Cole, in
his 'Essay on American Scenery' (1835), insists that 'the
wilderness is YET a fitting place to speak of God'. Against
those who prefer Europe, Cole argues that 'the most impressive characteristic of American scenery is its wildness',
while in 'civilized Europe the primitive features of scenery
have long since been destroyed or modified'. He instances
some of the splendid wildnesses of America, for example Niagara: 'in gazing on it we feel as though a great void had
been filled in our mind—our conceptions expand—we become a part of what we behold'. (It is amusing to recall that
when Chateaubriand first saw Niagara he was so over-
whelmed that he wanted to throw himself in, and indeed did
nearly fall over the edge—a pregnant Romantic anecdote.
And it was in the wild American woods, Chateaubriand says,
a new, an 'unknown muse appeared to me'. Such wildness,
he felt, would provoke a new poetry.) At the same time anyone writing in America then was aware that the rapid 'im-
provements of cultivation' were inevitably replacing 'the
sublimity of the wilderness'. Here was a difficulty. The
American wilderness was a source of visionary exaltation.
Unlike Europe, the land was not scarred and stained by the
intolerable crimes of history: 'You see no ruined tower to tell
of outrage—no gorgeous temple to speak of ostentation.' But
if American landscape was not suffused with a sense of the
past it was full of what Cole calls 'associations . . . of the present and future'. 'And in looking over the yet uncultivated
scene, the mind's eye shall see far into futurity. Where the
wolf roams, the plough shall glisten; on the gray crag shall
rise temple and tower . . .' There is a problem for the American Romantic. Blessedly, there are no man-made towers
marring the American landscape; but happily there will
soon be towers springing up. The wonder and richness of
America is its wildness but wonderfully, the wildness will
soon be put to the plough. As soon as Cole has outlined his
optimistic vision of a civilized society living in a domesti-
cated landscape, he goes on 'yet I cannot but express my sorrow that the beauties of such landscapes are quickly passing
away—the ravages of the axe are daily increasing—the most
noble scenes are made desolate and oftentimes with a wan-

tonness and barbarism scarcely credible in a civilized nation'. Where the European Romantic, used to the 'traces of
men', might look forward to an imagined millennium for
human society, the American was very aware of increasing
depredations of the precious wildness. He might cling to images of idealized pastoral domesticity, or indulge in pieties
about manifest destiny or the melting-pot, but his strategy
on the whole was to seek out that solitude, those unpeopled
landscapes, prescribed by Emerson—in reality, or in art.
That is why while European Romanticism characteristically
looks to the past and to the future, American Romanticism
seeks to move out of time altogether, out of time and into
some sort of space. For time means history, and history
means 'traces of men' and society, and society means not
only the loss of 'that wilder image' but also the spaces it provided and the limitless freedom to sport in air. . . .

For good or bad the American Romantic writers do not
have that sense of the past which was so important for their
European counterparts. Of course, they faced a landscape
devoid of 'traces of men': clean, 'dazzling', but humanly
speaking empty—potentially alien in a way that the European landscape, so saturated with history, legend, myth,
could never be. This perhaps partially explains why the European writer can seem to be more genuinely intimate with
his landscape than the American with his, why it offers him
so much in the way of suggestions, associations, and conso-
lations, while the American landscape, 'that wilder image',
tends to hold off from its watcher as pure obdurate fact. Of
course there is a whole tradition of sublime writing cele-
brating nature in American Romantic poetry. Josephine
Miles has described it in her excellent *Eras and Modes in English Poetry* (London, 1977), but she also, most interestingly,
notes that the whole vocabulary of subtle 'psychological dis-
criminations' which was developed by the English Romantics was not adopted or developed in America. This corresponds to my sense that the American Romantic feels nature
to be something so vast as to be almost beyond him; he does
not feel that sort of psychological intimacy with his environment, that sense of reciprocities between man and man, man
and nature, which marks much European Romantic writing.
For Emerson, despite his celebratory euphoria, the actual
surrounding world could often seem 'an Iceland of negations' from which he would habitually escape into his vi-

sions of 'infinitude'. Similarly, Wallace Stevens uses the image of a barren wintry landscape to describe his sense of a world which has not been supplemented and illuminated by some imaginary construct invented by the poet himself. The world unmediated or unmodified by Imagination is perhaps a cold and empty place for most Romantics. But whereas the European seems to draw help from history, legend, memory, from friends (and lovers), from visions of future societies, from the landscape itself, as he strives to fill that emptiness, the American Romantic seems to be thrown back much more on his own resources, the devices and designs of his own style. To consider American Romantic literature from Emerson to Wallace Stevens in this light is to realize anew how very remarkable and inventive those resources are.

That recurrent image of the spider, drawing the filament out of himself alone, weaving his private web, provides an illuminating analogy for the situation, and secretion, of the American writer. His delight (or is it sometimes his desperation?) is to put together his own unique verbal structure; and in this activity, the ingredients which go into the making of each piece of filament are perhaps less important than the fact of the web itself which sustains the writer in the real and imagined spaces of America. The visions of the European Romantic interpenetrated on all sides with their natural and human surroundings. It is just this feeling of *interpenetration* that seems to me to be missing in the work of the American Romantic. If we seek him out we are most likely to find him as Emily Dickinson found her spider—dancing softly to himself, unwinding his coil of Pearl. The wonder is what 'continents of light' he thus manages to summon into being.

CHAPTER 4

The Individual in American Romanticism

American
Romanticism

Thoreau: The Individual Versus the Institution

Michael J. Hoffman

Michael J. Hoffman is a professor of English at the University of California at Davis and the author of several books of literary criticism. In the following selection, excerpted from his book *The Subversive Vision: American Romanticism in Literature*, he discusses Henry David Thoreau's belief that society restricted the freedoms of the individual.

The central dilemma running throughout Romanticism is the sundering of self and role. If pre-Romantic man felt that society had either a divine or a rationalistic foundation and that his own sense of identity sprang from both this society and from a universal order controlled by a deity or by immutable laws, then he could ultimately feel no conflict between himself as an individual sentient being and himself as player of a social role. He had no sense, in other words, of "playing a role."

Romantic consciousness forced nineteenth-century man to realize both that he had an inner core of identity independent of the world outside his consciousness and that playing a social role violated this inner sense of selfhood. It is the feeling of being violated by an inimical society that lies at the root of Romantic alienation. And yet, if alienation began as an emotional reaction, it also became something of a role in itself, played at one time or another by all the major Romantic figures. To be the outcast, the exploited outsider who is violated by an unsympathetic, impersonal society, was a stance familiar to most major figures of the nineteenth century. Indeed, alienation is today a necessary rite of passage for anyone who wishes to qualify as a "modern" individual. But alienation is not a final stage: it is the phase associated

Excerpted from Michael J. Hoffman, *The Subversive Vision: American Romanticism in Literature*. (Port Washington, NY: Kennikat Press, 1972.) Reprinted with permission from the author. (Footnotes in the original have been omitted from this reprint.)

most often with Negative Romanticism. Although all Romantic figures seem to move at some time in their lives through Negative Romantic isolation and alienation, most figures in English literature after Byron and in American literature after Poe find ways to go beyond this early disillusionment in order to reassert the self and to restructure society.

Of all the classic figures of the "American Renaissance" no one felt so radically alienated as Thoreau. In what is still one of the best studies of his thought Joseph Wood Krutch documents Thoreau's cultivation of an almost doctrinal antipathy to the structures of middle-class life and the government that represented it. But even Krutch did not show the depth of Thoreau's commitment to developing many of the traditional Romantic positions in relation to the individual and society.

Thoreau's commitment to Romanticism may be seen by examining . . . "Civil Disobedience," his classic essay on militant nonviolence. . . .

The widespread influence of this legendary speech is well known. Tolstoy, Gandhi, and Martin Luther King, all found it an extraordinary expression of conscience and individual integrity in the face of an oppressive government. For a Transcendentalist all social structures can become oppressive institutions—even fashion in clothing. An examination of "Civil Disobedience" will reveal its close parallels to Thoreau's later statements in *Walden*. The man of letters and the polemicist are two aspects of the same organic self.

If there is any fundamental truth for Transcendentalism, it is that the ground beneath "reality" is spiritual. As in *Nature*, if all individuals draw their being from the same spiritual source, and if spirit is moral, then the most important actions, the only "real" actions, are moral choices. The individual knows whether he is right or wrong because of his "conscience." Though conscience is usually described as being socially trained (much like Freud's superego), Emerson and Thoreau find it to be rooted in that innate spiritual bond between man and all material creation, and they contend that man knows through intuition the differences between right and wrong moral choices. The difficulties of this position are obvious; but the logical conclusion drawn is that, if all things are moral, and if they must thereby have an immediate, direct relationship to spiritual reality, then man must reject anything at all that has a stench of moral expediency, be it clothing or government.

GOVERNMENTS THREATEN THE
INDIVIDUAL'S MORAL INTEGRITY

Thoreau notes almost immediately that "Government is at best but an expedient; but most governments are usually, and all governments are sometimes, inexpedient." Governments, like all institutions, are established to control behavioral ambiguity by reducing the individual's choices. In order even to live in a complex society, people must delegate much moral authority elsewhere, so that they will not have to spend all their time simply coping with survival. This, at least, is how governments begin. Later events, however, differ; for governments, like all institutions, obey the iron law of self-perpetuation, and survival has no connection with moral choice; it only relates to survival. In fact, moral decisions are often inexpedient to the functioning of any institution. That is why Thoreau begins his speech-essay by quoting the statement, "That government is best which governs least," which he then modifies to "not at all." Governments, like all institutions, are necessarily organs of expedience, and as such they constantly threaten the individual's moral integrity by involving him in their necessary compromises. It is important to understand the Transcendentalist assumptions on the basis of which Thoreau attacks the American government.

Thoreau shows his contempt for men in the mass when he states of the government:

> It has not the vitality and force of a single living man; for a single man can bend it to his will. It is a sort of wooden gun to the people themselves. But it is not the less necessary for this; for the people must have some complicated machinery or other, and hear its din, to satisfy that idea of government which they have.

Mass man gives over his soul—his powers of moral decision—to a mob that follows conditioned responses rather than the dictates of universal spirit. It is men in the mass who have perverted the democratic ideal by insisting that they as a "majority" have the right to control the lives and moral choices of everyone else. "Can there not be a government in which majorities do not virtually decide right and wrong, but conscience?" But the question answers itself. How can governments, which need great crowds of people simply to keep their machinery whirling, make decisions of conscience? Only individuals can make moral distinctions;

and as soon as two individuals incorporate, the possibility is instantaneously diminished that either one will make a decision consistent with spiritual truth. Furthermore, most individuals like the situation as it stands. Because the need to make choices is existentially frightening, most men spend their lives avoiding such necessities. In this avoidance they find a more than willing ally in their government, which gives men a small illusion of participatory freedom in order to convince them that they control their own destinies, whereas in reality it has stolen their moral sense completely.

The instrument used by the government and all institutions to maintain their power and the status quo is that of the law. By creating the illusion that justice is being served through law, governments can once again manipulate this illusion to control their constituents. Like most Romantic writers, Thoreau scorns such deception:

> Law never made men a whit more just; and, by means of their respect for it, even the well-disposed are daily made the agents of injustice.

If law is the instrument of the state, and if the state represents either those with the most power or those in the majority, then it can have no relation to any abstract sense of justice: "The lawyer's truth is not Truth, but consistency or a consistent expedience."

THE INDIVIDUAL'S DUTY

Thoreau goes on, in a vein that prefigures Herbert Marcuse's essay on "Repressive Tolerance," to note that the individual who simply goes along with the state, without either sponsoring or actively engaging in its injustices, who in the name of order obeys the laws because not to do so would be tantamount to anarchy, is just as guilty as the man who partakes directly in the actions of the government. There is no such thing as an uninvolved man, for moral choice consists in taking positive action. "Even voting *for the right,*" Thoreau claims, "is *doing* nothing for it. It is only expressing to men feebly your desire that it should prevail." Voting, even if it means voting on the correct side of any issue, still constitutes working within the system. Reform, by which Thoreau means ethical change, can come only from people who assert their moral individuality and who, by doing so, break with established institutional channels.

Those who, while they disapprove of the character and measures of a government, yield to it their allegiance and support are undoubtedly its most conscientious supporters, and so frequently the most serious obstacles to reform.

The truly moral man must disregard his government whenever necessary; he must even, if necessary, "break the law" in order to allow his life to "be a counter-friction to stop the machine." The important thing is to be on the side of the right and not that of a majority, for "any man more right than his neighbors constitutes a majority of one already."

THE UNJUSTNESS OF GOVERNMENT

Unjust laws exist; shall we be content to obey them, or shall we endeavor to amend them, and obey them until we have succeeded, or shall we transgress them at once? Men generally, under such a government as this, think that they ought to wait until they have persuaded the majority to alter them. They think that, if they should resist, the remedy would be worse than the evil. But it is the fault of the government itself that the remedy *is* worse than the evil. *It* makes it worse. Why is it not more apt to anticipate and provide for reform? Why does it not cherish its wise minority? Why does it cry and resist before it is hurt? Why does it not encourage its citizens to be on the alert to point out its faults, and *do* better than it would have them? Why does it always crucify Christ, and excommunicate Copernicus and Luther, and pronounce Washington and Franklin rebels?

Henry David Thoreau, *Civil Disobedience*, 1849.

Like most moral absolutists, Thoreau knew himself to be always on the side of the right. Whether or not this accusation is legitimate, its sources can be understood to lie in Transcendentalist metaphysics; Thoreau dramatizes a moral dilemma that has not yet been solved. Even if he is arrogant in assuming his own rightness, he also shows keen insight in pointing out that men cannot consider themselves moral beings if they give over their consciences to the nearest institution. Thoreau, as an individual who is cognizant of the dangers inherent in representative democracy, is entitled by Transcendentalist assumptions to assert that "Under a government which imprisons any unjustly, the true place for a just man is also a prison." It is a statement that prepares the way for Eugene Debs [American socialist leader and activist in the labor movement of the 1890s] as well as for contemporary resistance movements.

Thoreau's digressions are as illuminating as his main points about the government, and they are ultimately just as much to the point. He speaks of money as an institution that binds a man to it and that controls his moral integrity as much as any government:

> If there were one who lived wholly without the use of money, the State itself would hesitate to demand it of him. But the rich man—not to make any invidious comparison—is always sold to the institution which makes him rich. Absolutely speaking, the more money, the less virtue.

The echoes of Christian asceticism here are not assertions of Christlike piety. Thoreau sees money not merely as an instrument of the devil; he views money and the love of it as a symptom of the middle-class life that invests its energies, not in moral and spiritual capital, but in material accumulation. And the more a man accumulates, the more he needs the protection of governments, armies, and police. It is not simple perversity, antibourgeois paranoia, or anticapitalist asceticism that make Thoreau take such a stance. There is general agreement about the difficulty of remaining idealistic with an accumulation of property, money, and position. "The best thing a man can do for his culture when he is rich," Thoreau notes ironically, "is to endeavor to carry out those schemes which he entertained when he was poor." It is important to realize once again that he sees money and all its surrounding ramifications as institutions that perpetuate themselves by restricting moral choice.

THE ULTIMATE FOUNDATION OF GOVERNMENT

When Thoreau was put in jail for refusing to pay his poll tax, he learned that force is the ultimate foundation of a government. The government is not necessarily rational, although it does create laws to rationalize its operations. What it must do, however, when a citizen refuses it his money or his allegiance—even though the government is supposed to *represent* that very citizen—is either to coerce him into obeying or punish him for refusing. Thoreau's defense against being jailed is ridicule:

> I could not help being struck with the foolishness of that institution which treated me as if I were mere flesh and blood and bones, to be locked up. . . . As they could not reach me,

they had resolved to punish my body.

> Thus the state never intentionally confronts a man's sense, intellectual or moral, but only his body, his senses. It is not armed with superior wit or honesty, but with superior physical strength.

For Thoreau and the Transcendentalists, a man is more than his body or his sentient being. Because he is basically a creature of spirit, mind, and conscience, the mere detention of his body means nothing. It is a testimony to human superficiality that most people view being placed behind bars as tantamount to being destroyed, whereas it should be no more than an annoyance or perhaps even, as Thoreau takes pains to show, a doorway into a set of new experiences and insights. Thoreau describes his cell as being the cleanest and most freshly painted room in town. The jail was the one place in Concord where verses were composed. Thoreau claims that prison actually afforded him a new perspective on the world. By taking such an attitude, he turns the state's punishment into a positive experience. But could a "good citizen" have done so?

Thoreau manages this moral victory because he identifies himself completely within the context of Transcendentalist individualism. He refuses to be classified as part of a mass citizenry, and he pointedly resigns from any society he has not willingly and consciously joined:

> I am not responsible for the successful working of the machinery of society. I am not the son of the engineer. I perceive that, when an acorn and a chestnut fall side by side, the one does not remain inert to make way for the other, but both obey their own rules, and spring and grow and flourish as best they can, till one, perchance, overshadows and destroys the other. If a plant cannot live according to its nature, it dies; and so a man.

Whitman's Individualism

Newton Arvin

In the selection that follows, which was excerpted from the book *American Pantheon,* Newton Arvin challenges the view that Walt Whitman was an individualist. Although Whitman sympathized with the philosophy of individualism, Arvin contends, his work demonstrates a concern for society as a whole. Arvin is a famous literary critic and the author of several books on the American Romantic writers, including Nathaniel Hawthorne, Henry Wadsworth Longfellow, Walt Whitman, and Herman Melville.

Liberal and individualist critics are naturally inclined to read undiluted liberalism and individualism into whatever writers they find praiseworthy; and American critics of this stamp have pretty effectually put together an acceptable portrait of Walt Whitman out of their own range of pastel shades. According to this portrait, Whitman was merely the jolly and complacent spokesman of American middle-class democracy, undiscriminating, uncritically affirmative, and committed to the dogmas of self-help and self-expression in their simplest and even crudest form. The late Stuart Sherman, who admired Carnegie and his peers so cordially ("wholeheartedly and aspiringly democratic in their ends" as they were), once declared that "If Whitman had lived at the right place in these years of the Proletarian Millennium, he would have been hanged as a reactionary member of the bourgeoisie." [According to] Dr. H.S. Canby, "Walt never wrote for classes; the idea of a world proletariat based on economic grounds would have been repugnant to him. He wrote for individuals." There is, according to these critics, no dynamite in Whitman: there is indeed nothing in him that would not be acceptable to Herbert Hoover or, at least, to Governor Ritchie

Excerpted from Newton Arvin, *American Pantheon* (New York: Delacorte Press, 1966). Originally appeared in *The New Republic.*

[governor of Maryland during the 1920s who was known for his conservative, "law and order" approach to governing].

Certainly it is true that Whitman, as a preacher of self-reliance, had gone to school to Thomas Carlyle and Ralph Waldo Emerson; certainly it is true that, as a democrat, he had gone to school to Thomas Paine and Andrew Jackson and, later, Abraham Lincoln. If he was a radical, it is easy to show that his was in its origins the old American radicalism, and that he never completely abandoned his early Jeffersonian conviction that "that government is best which governs least." The man who stumped, in his youth, for Martin Van Buren and, in his old age, cherished the memory of his glimpses of Jackson, can hardly be made out to have been, body and soul, a twentieth-century collectivist. Yet is this equivalent to saying that there were not vital contradictions in his thought? that he gave expression to but one aspect of social history in the nineteenth century, and is now to be archaized by its passing? that the increasingly sharp antitheses in American society, as his life went on, made no appeal to his imagination, and had no effect on his work? Did he accept his own individualism without correction? Was he unaware that American business and American democracy were possibly at odds? Was his attitude toward social change simply that, in the good Sherman's phrase, of "a reactionary member of the bourgeoisie"? The true answers to these questions deserve a volume: I can only suggest what form they might take.

Dr. Canby has said that Whitman wrote only for individuals, never for classes; and that the idea of a world proletariat would be repugnant to him. Has Dr. Canby never looked through [Horace] Traubel's three volumes, *With Walt Whitman in Camden?* If so, was he not struck by a speech of Whitman's to his young friend on June 8, 1888? "Literature," said the old man, "is big only in one way—when used as an aid in the growth of the humanities—a furthering of the cause of the masses—a means whereby men may be revealed to each other as brothers." And a few months later, when Traubel had outlined to him Leo Tolstoy's notoriously anti-individualistic views on the arts, Whitman exclaimed: "I endorse them: O yes, with ten thousand times ten thousand amens: and if he goes on like that talking about the arts then you may say anywhere for me: Walt Whitman is with Tolstoy—count him in." These are scarcely the pronounce-

ments of a man who can justly be said to have written only
for individuals; and, as regards a world proletariat, one won-
ders how "repugnant" the idea would have been to the man
who said, in "A Backward Glance" (1888), "Without yielding
an inch the working man and working woman were to be in
my pages from first to last"; and who had already envisaged
the onrush of an internationalism which does not sound, in
his lines, like that of the League of Nations:

> Never was average man, his soul, more energetic, more like
>   a God,
> Lo, how he urges and urges, leaving the masses no rest! . . .
> Are all nations communing? is there going to be but one
>   heart to the globe?
> Is humanity forming en-masse?

WHITMAN'S CAREER IN PERSPECTIVE

But, indeed, to rely on particular citations such as these is to
do the question injustice: it need not rest upon them. Quite
aside from single phrases in his prose or verse, or the oracles of his old age, it is possible to see Whitman's "individualistic" radicalism in its true light by focusing his whole career in perspective. It is true that he was a transcendental
egoist who had sat at the feet of Emerson, and was in sympathy with the expansive individualism of the middle
decades of the century; true that he believed that "The
American compact is altogether with individuals"; true that
he came too early to have any grasp of historical materialism, or to see social history in terms of a struggle between
classes. But there is a radical paradox in his work, as there
was in his age, and, for all his egoism, his real sympathies
were intensely democratic; his individualism, unlike Emerson's, was profoundly modified by his gospel of comradeship and solidarity; unlike most of his contemporaries, he
was violently critical, from the beginning, of the individualism of business enterprise; and, even before the Civil War,
certainly in the years that followed, he saw with remarkable
clarity that American democracy had much of tragic implication to fear from the greed of predatory individuals. He
was born too soon to make, in his own imagination, the
transition from Thomas Paine to Karl Marx; but, in his old
age, in conversation, he spoke far more in the manner of a
Marxian than of a Jacksonian; and Traubel, who was a Socialist, had little difficulty in persuading the old poet to con-

cur with his opinions, at least in general terms.

Jacksonian as a young newspaper editor he may have been, but the democracy that comes out in his editorials in *The Brooklyn Eagle* (1846–47) or in reprinted editorials from *The Brooklyn Daily Times* (1857–59) is by no means merely the democracy of Van Buren, Cass and Polk, or of Pierce and Buchanan. His remarks in *The Eagle* on wage cuts in the white-lead factories in Brooklyn, or on the effects of slavery in degrading white workers as well as black, or on protection ("Has any one of our laboring fellow citizens such thin perceptions—does he imagine in his most abstracted dreams—that all this hubbub made by the pale-fingered richly housed Whig manufacturers, and their organs, is for *him*, the laborer?"), or on the profit-motive ("Our American capitalists of the manufacturing order, would *poor* a great many people to be rich!")—such remarks as these may be the remarks of an individualist, but only, surely, of a critical one. . . .

On the horrors of unemployment during the panic of 1857, on "the gaunt physical want" of the city poor ("Down Below"), on the "greater reforms needed here [in the North] than in the Southern States," on the real meaning of the slavery evil ("the great cause of American White Work and Working people"), Whitman is quite as eloquent as on the civic advantages of Brooklyn and the laying of the Atlantic cable.

WHITMAN'S DISENCHANTMENT WITH DEMOCRACY

Yet it was only after the war, when the patriotic emotions stimulated by that crisis had begun to subside, that Whitman was first seriously and painfully agitated by the gloomy contradictions of American democracy, and only in "Democratic Vistas" that he first allowed himself to formulate his anxieties explicitly. "The depravity of the business classes of our country," he there protested, "is not less than has been supposed, but infinitely greater. . . . In business (this all-devouring modern word, business) the one sole object is, by any means, pecuniary gain." He admonished his countrymen not to ignore "that problem, the labor question, beginning to open like a yawning gulf, rapidly widening every year"; and reminded them that for them, too, "as for all lands," there existed "the wily person in office, scrofulous wealth, the surfeit of prosperity, the demonism of greed . . . the fossil-like lethargy, the ceaseless need of revolutions." Later, as the depression of the seventies, stretching out blackly from year to year, exposed the inevitable underside of American prosperity, Whitman came more and more to see how profoundly the basis of democracy was shifting; and in such fragments as "The Tramp and Strike Questions" ("not the abstract question of democracy, but of social and economic organization, the treatment of working people by employers"), "Who Gets the Plunder?" and "Central Park Notes" (notes printed in *Collect* and *November Boughs*) he confessed that his youthful confidence in the happy future of American democracy had had to be qualified by experience.

By the late eighties, when Traubel began his diary record, Whitman's political and social views had settled down to a consistent level of bitter and disappointed, though never hopeless, protest against the dirtiness of American politics, the corruption of both the Republican and Democratic parties ("these damned huckster parties"), the unscrupulousness of American capital, and the venality of church and press. Speaking of slavery, he once said: "I never could quite lose the sense of other evils in this evil—I saw other evils that cried to me in perhaps even a louder voice: the labor evil, now, to speak of only one, which to this day has been steadily growing worse, worse, worse." "I am not interested," he said again, "in what Carnegie is doing to establish libraries abroad but in what he is doing to keep peace with and render justice to his men here." He clung to his old views of protection: "The protection of profit—the protection of the swell proprietors—I guess I don't care a shucks for that: I guess I'd just whip it out of the temple with cords any day if I could." The old journalist of the Greeley era realized what was happening to the newspapers: "They are all getting into the hands of millionaires. God help our liberties when money has finally got our institutions in its clutch." And the old free thinker realized what was happening to religion: "You spoke," said Traubel once, "of the priests of religion and the priests of the arts. We still have the priests of commerce to contend with." "So we have," replied Whitman: "doubly so: the priests of commerce augmented by the priests of churches, who are everywhere the parasites, the apologists, of systems as they exist."

HOPE FOR A TRANSFORMED SOCIETY

Such, in terms that he constantly recurred to, were Whitman's feelings about American capitalism in the eighties. He

was a mere individualist, say the liberal critics: did he, then,
go back on his old faith in the masses and betake himself to
the praise of "strong men," "heroes" and "rugged individuals"? Did he, on the other hand, abandon both democracy
and the hero, and relapse into senile despair? He did neither.
On the contrary, he reiterated his old democratic loyalties,
against the background of a transformed society, with a new
emphasis and a new zeal. "America," he said, "is not for special types, for the castes, but for the great mass of people—
the vast, surging, hopeful army of workers." Again, speaking
of some mechanics he knew fondly: "They, their like, the
crowd of the grave workingmen of our world—they are the
hope, the sole hope, the sufficient hope, of our democracy."
And still later:

> I liked what [Edward Carpenter] said of the mechanics at
> Leeds: I put my faith in them—in the crowd of every-day
> men—in the rise, the supremacy (not the rule) of the superb
> masses: the men who do things—the workers: they are our
> hope—they will lead us on if we are led on: not the kid-gloved
> nobses: . . . I don't see what they can do for us except lead
> wrong ways—to the devil—yes, lead us into a hole.

But what were such sentiments to lead to, in the future, in
the twentieth century? To socialism? He shrank, the old Free
Soiler, from committing himself quite irrevocably. "Lots of
it—lots—lots," he replied, however, when Traubel asked
him whether he had any sympathy with the Socialism of
William Morris; and, on another day:

> Sometimes I think, I feel almost sure, Socialism is the next
> thing coming: I shrink from it in some ways yet it looks like
> our only hope. I'm a sort of an anarchist tramp, too: and you?
> well, you are a lot like me . . . but things drive us on—the God
> damned robbers, fools, stupids, who ride their gay horses
> over the bodies of the crowd: they drive us on: God knows to
> what: sometimes I don't like to think of it: but they'll drive us
> into an inevitable resentment, then revolt, of some sort.

One day, when he was complaining that the many were
swindled by the few, Traubel asked him: "Do you think the
class that has robbed the people will hand their loot back?"
"I'm afraid not," he returned: "I'm afraid the people will have
to fight for what they get." "Why, Walt," cried his friend,
"you're a damned good revolutionist after all!" He was
amused, says Traubel. "Didn't you always know it? What
could I be if I wasn't?"

Such was the man who has been called a potential bourgeois reactionary, an old-fashioned Jacksonian democrat and the poet solely of individuals. It looks as if there were more dynamite in Whitman than the liberals have found in him. It looks as if, were he living today, his loyalties might be, not with the Shermans and Canbys, but with the men and women to whom he addressed himself at the beginning:

> You workwomen and workmen of these States having your
>   own divine and strong life,
> And all else giving place to men and women like you.

The Isolation of the Individual in *Moby-Dick*

Quentin Anderson

Quentin Anderson is the author of *The American Henry James, The Imperial Self: An Essay in American Literary and Cultural History*, and *Making Americans: An Essay on Individualism and Money*, from which the subsequent selection was excerpted. In this selection he explains how *Moby-Dick* reflects Herman Melville's belief that the individual is isolated from society.

Herman Melville early came to feel himself a loner, and even culturally orphaned; he was pressed when very young to ask ultimate questions about the human condition. Pushing all preachers aside, he looked into an abyss which seems to have opened for him as a consequence of the financial failure, madness, and death of his father. He felt himself cast adrift on the world, became a schoolteacher, and thereafter took a place still lower in the social order as a seaman before the mast. Although he was never without ties to more fortunate relatives or a touch of self-dramatizing awareness of his class origins, his voyages gave him a range of experience leagues beyond that of any other middle-class writer of his time. Mark Twain observes that he is seldom surprised by oddities of human character and behavior, since he had met such a multitude of human variations during his years as apprentice and pilot on the Mississippi; Melville had much more extensive grounds for claiming that he had encountered humanity in myriad guises under the most taxing conditions.

Melville's early literary success—*Typee* and *Omoo* were published when he was in his late twenties—seemed to overlie his sense of disaffiliation. Recognition in New York's literary coterie, publication in England, and an initially

Excerpted from Quentin Anderson, *Making Americans: An Essay on Individualism and Money*. (New York: Harcourt Brace Jovanovich, 1992.) Reprinted with the permission of the author.

happy marriage and fatherhood combined to make it appear that he was launched into a world prepared to receive him. The mixed reception of *Mardi*, in which his preoccupation with ultimate questions prevailed over the seagoing yarn with which it begins, made for a momentary hitch, which *Redburn* seemed to repair. But Melville was far too variously intelligent and too much the cosmopolitan to feel at ease with the terms on which he had been received. His readers were pleased by tales of the exotic South Seas or angered by his attacks on missionaries, but in his own view they altogether missed his larger intentions; he was being praised for dancing in puddles; few noticed that he had dived into deeper waters, or, if they did so, told him to get back to his job. When, after another attempt at conformity in *White Jacket*, Melville really let himself go in *Moby Dick* (1851), his star fell, never to rise again during his lifetime or in the thirty years following his death in 1891.

Melville's importance for this book lies in the fact that his sense of things differs both from that of those who find themselves socially surrounded and from that of the aspiring world possessors, Ralph Waldo Emerson, Henry David Thoreau, and Walt Whitman. He was neither able to believe that he had grown in a social medium nor moved to create an outsider's version of individual capacities to embrace existence. Alone in an arena constituted by the presence of other persons, who often agglomerated themselves into mobs, he struggled to preserve an identity, hunted by forces without and haunted by impulses which arose within. Melville took the world personally. As insistent as Emerson on the premise that each of us must shoulder the responsibility for interpreting existence and that institutions are but the shadows of those who profit by them, he is wholly persuaded that our identities are perennially at risk, that others have the power to invade us and deprive us of our full selfhood. He is adramatic in the sense that encounters don't alter relations between his fictional characters but rather issue in collisions which overcome the characters or enable them to swallow up other identities; his is a scene of instances; he is, like Emerson, Thoreau, and Whitman, an exemplary writer, but what he sees as our vulnerability cancels the Emersonian hope of arriving at a vision of things which neatly complements our inward powers. Melville shared the exemplary mode, which is essentially adramatic, without feeling assured that he could make the world square with his vision of it. What is viewed as a satire directed against Emerson and the practical consequences of Emersonianism in Melville's tale *The Confidence Man* (1857) amounts to condemnation of a desiccating impersonality which is as inhumane as the impersonality of ruthless money-getting. He makes bitter fun of the man who held that we can be friends with others only on the ground that they sympathize with our exalted spiritual aspirations. For Melville there was no such escape into abstraction; his was a world in which individuals encountered other individuals.

THE ISOLATED PEOPLE OF *MOBY DICK*

There is a pervasive oddity about *Moby Dick,* the book that has counted most heavily among us. The persons of this novel move about the decks almost as isolated from one another as so many sleepwalkers, who make of the people and objects they meet the subjects of their dreams. What qualifies this comparison is of course a shared absorption in the crafts of whaling and sailing a ship. Practice flows in to fill the vacancy of the middle ground of human intercourse. We are led to accept this because it accords with our sense of the strict regimen of shipboard existence, here intensified by the scorching will of Ahab. The effect is pervasively felt, so that snatches of colloquies and inner ruminations seem like murmurs among the groundlings who catch only distant glimpses of the cosmic spectacle which Ahab and Ishmael are in different ways confronted by. It often seems that each speaks out of his own isolate preoccupation. The illustrative set piece is of course the series of quite distinct reflections on the doubloon Ahab nails to the mast as a prize for the first sighting of Moby Dick. The two visionaries, Ishmael and Ahab, share the world of practice with the rest, but they alone, barely limited by the presence of others, press toward ultimate judgments of the human condition.

The interactions between characters don't have the property of shaping events and determining actions; they too have the character of illustrative generality. Before Ishmael and Queequeg board the ship one may cling to the notion that one is reading a conventional narrative. Once on board, if we except the tie between Ishmael and Queequeg, the expectation of such a narrative diminishes. Conversations between Ahab and the carpenter, Ahab and Pip, Ahab and Starbuck exemplify dissonances in the way experience is construed by each character, although Ahab has the power to constrain the behavior of all of them. We find such snatches of narrative as do crop up chiefly in passages which deal with encounters with other whalers. These serve to highlight the social vacuity of the *Pequod;* intertwined human needs and purposes reach its decks from other ships but in that vacuum gasp and die like so many flying fish landing on deck. The ship's crew, through whom the impulses of Ahab's will dart like electrical shocks, seem not to share any collective awareness, save in the surreal Shakespeareanizing of "The Forecastle at Midnight" (chapter 39).

Given our sense of the separateness and isolation which attend the putative "characters" on board, how are we to see them as constrained to sail on the same ship, or to appear on the same page? One is led to feel that they do so only as manifestations within the consciousness of Ishmael or in that consciousness to which we must submit as long as Ishmael does, that of Ahab. The others do not—again with the exception of Queequeg's bond with Ishmael—contribute to a developing action of which they are a part because they seem mere appearances fleetingly entertained by Ishmael and Ahab. Even Stubb's cruel taunting of the cook about the preparation of a delicate portion of whale meat suggests that the cook is simply a foil for Stubb's exhibition of what goes on in his head, a miniature reduplication of the ampler appropriation of the existence of others in the consciousness of the visionary characters, Ishmael and Ahab. The reader in turn must wholly submit to Ishmael; he is master of our awareness. It would be ridiculous, for example, to call him the "hero" of the book we are reading, because others appear to him as aspects of an inclusive reality rather than agents on a scene he shares with them.

Those who seek or claim a global reach for their sense of things are minimally associated with the conventional uses of the term "character" in fiction. Yet Ahab, who has such a world-engrossing vision, has undertaken to be an agent, an actor on the universal scene he has envisaged. He has turned a commercial venture into a quest as fantastic as that of Gilgamesh in pursuit of immortality. Extrapolating the absolute authority conferred on the captain of a ship, he conscripts his crew as accessories of his fantasy and hunts down a beast which personifies all that is irrevocable in human existence.

If Ishmael, both comprehending witness and threatened individual, were not present the book would hardly engage the
reader; it would simply be a fable about a mad sea captain
who tries to avenge the loss of a leg to a sperm whale.

MELVILLE'S CONCEPTION OF INDIVIDUAL EXISTENCE

The part played by Ishmael in *Moby Dick* affords the best example of Melville's conception of individual existence. The
devil-may-care Ishmael whom the reader first meets takes
to the sea as an alternative to "pistol and ball," that is, sui-
cide; he is at odds with himself and the world. He alone of
those who board the *Pequod* is prepared to apprehend the
pitch of desperation which leads Ahab to aggregate all human ills in Moby Dick and seek to destroy them, as if the
whale was the incarnation of whatever was adverse to humanity. This project can only be referred to as an effort to
enact a metaphor. Since whales had in fact been known to
attack ships, the action of the whale in the story represents
no breach with possibility, but it does take an Ishmael or his
fellow to give the yarn significance for the reader, since his
is the only consciousness capable of embracing the measure
of Ahab's colossal disaffection. When you attempt to univer-
salize your relation to the world, as Ahab does, human others recede, become bit players in the mythology you are creating. Because Ishmael too has been impelled to ask
inclusive questions about the meaning of existence, he is
vulnerable to the peculiar grandeur of Ahab's legend. He is
also fearful of the consequences of a voyage on a ship "rushing from all havens astern."

What distinguishes Ishmael from all other major characters in Melville's work is simply his points of attachment to
the world, to his "dear Pacific," to which he writes a paean,
to the spectacle of the whale nursery, to his pleasure in
everything in nature that beguiles him. One might almost
call him Emersonian, until we realize that "nature" is never
the self's all-inclusive window on the world for him; his is
the natural world of a particular sensibility with chosen
loves, and he is wary all the while of its dangers. Melville
does not, in most of his work, give this much weight to such
moments of rejoicing in the being of the world; Ishmael's capacity for pleasure is significant by contrast, and his relatively assured sense of his situation is not found elsewhere
in Melville's writings.

What sort of man is Ishmael? An acquaintance with the bulk of Melville's work makes this question loom because this extraordinarily loquacious character, whose address to us makes up much of *Moby Dick,* seems almost assimilated to the exercise of telling us about whaling and the voyage of the *Pequod, so* that we find it difficult to conceive of his having had a precedent life or a subsequent one. More important still is the unparalleled exuberance he shows in universalizing his immediate experience in the book. His emphasis on the way he takes the sensations that pleasure him, frighten him, shock him—the degree to which he is played upon by the world instead of trying to shape it—might lead us to compare him to a blank canvas which images and ideas are unremittingly filling in, or to a participant observer reporting on the passions, skills, and employment of the cultural artifacts of his own species.

Is it extravagant to say then that *Moby Dick* seems to be what happens *in* Ishmael? That he is aestheticizing his response to what happens to him in order to incorporate it? If so, in what way does he differ from the conventional narrator? Ishmael's account of the composition of the crew, now "federated along one keel," emphasizes a separateness, a fortress-like apartness. "They were nearly all Islanders in the *Pequod. Isolatoes* too, I call such, not acknowledging the common continent of men, but each *Isolato* living on a separate continent of his own." The matter-of-fact statement of the crew's origins immediately gives way to Ishmael's characteristic emphasis on the isolation of individual consciousness, of which he is the prime example, although to us he talks all the while. So again, in the chapter called "The Mat-Maker," we find him saying, "such an incantation of revery lurked in the air that each silent sailor seemed resolved into his invisible self."

Ishmael departs from the stance of the conventional narrator by appealing to those who feel themselves sundered from society—to those as isolated as himself. No such audience had yet been constituted; few people were prepared to read Melville's book at the moment of its publication. Only later would Americans feel alone enough to accept it. An acute reviewer of *Typee,* Melville's first novel, had made a stab at suggesting that Melville had cut himself off from any existing audience in portions of that book. Failing to notice the desperation which leads the hero to flee from the

Typees, he nonetheless calls Melville a traitor to his western kind: "He [Melville] writes of what he has seen *con amore,* and at times almost loses his loyalty to civilization and the Anglo-Saxon race."

The exuberance of the prose with which Melville endows Ishmael, a voice sounding like a trumpet at the gates of other fortress selves imagined as similarly responsive to a rendering of the universal plight—aware of their isolation and unbounded by "civilization"—must have been the product of the high-water mark of the writer's personal integration. In this book Melville's writing masters a split in his sense of himself which shows in much of his other work. His Ishmael is both witness to and participant in an enterprise which serves to figure not civilization but the human condition at large as Melville conceives it. We can hardly account for his triumph as a writer, but it is possible to point to some of the contributing aspects of his success in this instance.

THE SELF IN SOCIETY

To write in what I have called the exemplary mode common to Emerson, Thoreau, Whitman, and Melville is to write from a conviction that the self, whether for good or ill, for enlightenment or ignorance, is the sole judge of our experience. The opposing view may be suggested by [literary critic] Kenneth Burke's term "dramatism," which entails a growth of our sense of things grounded in interplay with others. My contention here is concisely stated by Diana Trilling in the Foreword to a collection of her essays: "Far from believing that the self is best comprehended or realized apart from society, I am of the older opinion that it is society which provides the self with its best possibilities of ascendancy, even of transcendence. My opinion includes the belief that when we are implicated in society we are the more, not the less, likely to exist in all our personal variousness; . . ." Since these sentences were published, in 1964, our conception of something we might call "society" has grown more attenuated. The power of market economies over our minds and hearts has been ever more deeply interfused with our sense of things, but the root contention that the growth of distinctive individuals takes place in relation to the presence and influence of others remains, I assume, inescapable.

Melville, however, had little interest in the process of growing up which such a conviction involves, yet he remained free of the claim that the self could create a world congruent with its vision. The grounds on which, isolato that he was, he nonetheless resisted the Emersonian claim to the self's sufficiency arose from his sense that the integrity of his being was threatened by the power of others, expressed through force, or arbitrary authority, and the command of wealth, and by his own deepest erotic need: a loving tie with another man. He felt himself an outsider on both counts and wrote as if on guard against threats, studied other men for dear life, took the world personally because he was beset from within and without.

Emerson's Vision of the Self

Evan Carton

In the following selection, Evan Carton discusses
Ralph Waldo Emerson's vision of the relationship between nature, art, and the originality of the self. Carton, a professor of English at the University of Texas
at Austin, is the author of two books of literary criti-
cisms: *The Marble Faun: Hawthorne's Transformation*
and *The Rhetoric of American Romance: Dialectic and
Identity in Emerson, Dickinson, Poe, and Hawthorne*,
from which the following excerpt was taken.

"Why should not we also enjoy an original relation to the
universe?" In the fifth sentence of *Nature*, Ralph Waldo
Emerson makes, and goes on aggressively to elucidate, this
central demand. Originality means the curtailment of "ret-
rospective" tendencies and the development of a vigorous
commitment to immediacy, novelty, and personal achievement ("There are new lands, new men, new thoughts. Let us
demand our own works and laws and worship.") It is mani-
fested in "a poetry and philosophy of insight," and in "action
proportioned to nature." Originality, in Emerson's opening
paragraph, seems synonymous with creative self-assertion.

The rest of *Nature* offers considerable support for the initial suggestion that "an original relation to the universe" involves the activity of will and imagination—involves art.
Early on, Emerson affirms "a property in the horizon which
no man has but he whose eye can integrate all the parts, that
is, the poet." In contrast to ordinary landlords, who have
purchased or inherited physically bounded fields, the poet
entitles himself to property in the abstract when he takes
earth and sky into his field of vision and thereby integrates
the parts of the horizon. His property may be shared without
apportionment; each individual is a potential full possessor

Excerpted from Evan Carton, *The Rhetoric of American Romance: Dialectic and Identity in Emerson, Dickinson, Poe, and Hawthorne*, pp. 30-33. ©1985 Johns Hopkins University Press. Reprinted with permission from the publisher.

from his own perspective and through his own visionary act:

> Every rational creature has all nature for his dowry and es-
> tate. It is his, if he will. He may divest himself of it; he may
> creep into a corner, and abdicate his kingdom, as most men
> do, but he is entitled to the world by his constitution. In pro-
> portion to the energy of his thought and will, he takes up the
> world into himself.

Emerson's pun on "constitution" here forcibly joins two distinct, and perhaps opposed, senses of originality, as it suggests both that man's title to the world is inherent and that
he must perform a deliberate creative act to redeem it.

The potential for individual perception and expression of
the world, and the role of will in its fulfillment, is re-
emphasized in a later passage of the essay:

> The exercise of the Will, or the lesson of power, is taught in
> every event. . . . Nature is thoroughly mediate. It is made to
> serve. It receives the dominion of man as meekly as the ass
> on which the Saviour rode. It offers all its kingdoms to man
> as the raw material which he may mould into what is useful.
> Man is never weary of working it up.

Here, man is an artist who freely molds the unlimited plastic material that nature supplies. In so doing, he both shapes
the material world and creates his own image, defines himself. For nature not only "wears the colors of the spirit" but
also shares the form of the creative self; this is Emerson's
implication when he writes that man "takes up the world
into himself," that the poet "esteems nature . . . as fluid, and
impresses his being thereon," and that "this feeble human
being . . . penetrate[s] the vast masses of nature with an in-
forming soul, and recognize[s] itself in their harmony."
Knowledge and power reside in the convergence of the personal and the universal, a convergence that these passages
suggest the individual may effect and embody. Their suggestion is reinforced in "The American Scholar," where
Emerson argues that "the deeper [a man] dives into his pri-
vatest, secretest presentiment, to his wonder he finds this is
the most acceptable, most public and universally true"; in
the Divinity School "Address," where a living Christianity
may be generated only by the preacher's conversion of his
own life into truth via the idiosyncrasy of his expression;
and again in *Nature*, where "the world becomes at last only
a realized will—the double of the man."

At play in *Nature* and throughout Emerson, however, is
another sense of the self's relation to the world which casts

the idea of originality, and the effort to embody it, in an altogether different light:

> The world . . . differs from the body in one important respect. It is not, like that, now subjected to the human will. Its serene order is inviolable by us. It is, therefore, to us, the present expositor of the divine mind. It is a fixed point whereby we may measure our departure.

The opposition between this representation of the world and others in the same essay is striking. Here, the world is already formed and impervious to human will rather than fluid and ready to be shaped by it; hardly the double of the man, it marks an original "fixed point" from which he has departed. Primacy and originality inhere only in the divine mind which the world expounds and which man must reapproach through self-abnegation. His convergence with nature thus takes on the character of an attempt to "purge the eyes" so that he may become a passive reader of her prewritten "text." "By degrees," Emerson writes, "we may come to know the primitive sense of the permanent objects of nature, so that the world shall be to us an open book, and every form significant of its hidden life and final cause."

When the individual stands divorced from nature's primitiveness and permanence, and from the world's "hidden life and final cause," and hopes to be initiated "by degrees," his only attitude is one of patience and receptivity. This, Emerson suggests in "Spiritual Laws," is historically the attitude of great men. They are as smooth and hollow as flutes; in them "that which externally seem[s] will and immovableness [is] willingness and self-annihilation." The concluding paragraph of "Circles" affirms such selflessness to be man's universal goal: "The one thing which we seek with insatiable desire is to forget ourselves, to be surprised out of our *propriety*, . . . and to do something without knowing how or why." [Emphasis added.] This last phrase recalls the "untaught sallies of the spirit" which Emerson recommends in *Nature* but which he characterizes as "a continual self-recovery." The polarization of the self and of the meaning of originality, for Emerson, is apparent from the earliest essays. Self-assertion is self-departure, self-annihilation is self-recovery. Occasionally Emerson seeks relief from the conceptual and linguistic tensions which this intrinsic antagonism produces and falls back on some version of the traditional Christian division of the self into body and soul, but this static solution holds little appeal for him. His forefathers' times and (as *Nature* insists) the forms appropriate to them have passed; besides, he has rejected their institutional religious context. Moreover, he has conceived his project as a quest to reunify man with himself, not to classify his fragments. Finally, he sees and feels the act of writing as an enterprise that engages the self in all its duality and, thus, may facilitate the self's achievement of a dynamic wholeness.

CHAPTER 5

Allegory and Symbolism

American
Romanticism

Poe's Motifs of Enclosure

Richard Wilbur

In the following selection, originally presented as a
lecture at the Library of Congress in 1959, poet and
literary critic Richard Wilbur discusses the role of
symbolism in the work of Edgar Allan Poe. According to Wilbur, Poe employs recurring motifs of enclosure—in particular, enclosure within houses and
rooms—to symbolize his characters' isolation from
the real world.

Edgar Allan Poe conceived of God as a poet. The universe,
therefore, was an artistic creation, a poem composed by
God. Now, if the universe is a poem, it follows that the one
proper response to it is aesthetic, and that God's creatures
are attuned to Him in proportion as their imaginations are
ravished by the beauty and harmony of his creation. Not to
worship beauty, not to regard poetic knowledge as divine,
would be to turn one's back on God and fall from grace.

The planet Earth, according to Poe's myth of the cosmos,
has done just this. It has fallen away from God by exalting
the scientific reason above poetic intuition, and by putting its
trust in material fact rather than in visionary knowledge.
The Earth's inhabitants are thus corrupted by rationalism
and materialism; their souls are diseased; and Poe sees this
disease of the human spirit as having contaminated physical
nature. The woods and fields and waters of Earth have
thereby lost their first beauty, and no longer clearly express
God's imagination; the landscape has lost its original perfection of composition, in proportion as men have lost their
power to perceive the beautiful.

Since Earth is a fallen planet, life upon Earth is necessarily a torment for the poet: neither in the human sphere nor
in the realm of nature can he find fit objects for contempla-

Excerpted from Richard Wilbur, "The House of Poe," 1959 Library of Congress Anniver-
sary Lecture, in *Romanticism: Critical Essays in American Literature,* edited by James
Barbour and Thomas Quirk. Reprinted with permission from Garland Publishing, Inc.

tion, and indeed his soul is oppressed by everything around him. The rationalist mocks at him; the dull, prosaic spirit of the age damps his imaginative spark; the gross materiality of the world crowds in upon him. His only recourse is to abandon all concern for Earthly things, and to devote himself as purely as possible to unearthly visions, in hopes of glimpsing that heavenly beauty which is the thought of God.

THE POETIC SOUL AT WAR

Poe, then, sees the poetic soul as at war with the mundane physical world; and that warfare is Poe's fundamental subject. But the war between soul and world is not the only war. There is also warfare within the poet's very nature. To be sure, the poet's nature was not always in conflict with itself. Prior to his earthly incarnation, and during his dreamy childhood, Poe's poet enjoyed a serene unity of being; his consciousness was purely imaginative, and he knew the universe for the divine poem that it is. But with his entrance into adult life, the poet became involved with a fallen world in which the physical, the factual, the rational, the prosaic are not escapable. Thus, compromised, he lost his perfect spirituality, and is now cursed with a divided nature. Though his imagination still yearns toward ideal beauty, his mortal body chains him to the physical and temporal and local; the hungers and passions of his body draw him toward external objects, and the conflict of conscience and desire degrades and distracts his soul; his mortal senses try to convince him of the reality of a material world which his soul struggles to escape; his reason urges him to acknowledge everyday fact, and to confine his thought within the prison of logic. For all these reasons it is not easy for the poet to detach his soul from earthly things, and regain his lost imaginative power—his power to commune with that supernal beauty which is symbolized, in Poe, by the shadowy and angelic figures of Ligeia, and Helen, and Lenore.

These, then, are Poe's great subjects: first, the war between the poetic soul and the external world; second, the war between the poetic soul and the earthly self to which it is bound. All of Poe's major stories are allegorical presentations of these conflicts, and everything he wrote bore somehow upon them.

How does one wage war against the external world? And how does one release one's visionary soul from the body, and from the constraint of the reason? These may sound like difficult tasks; and yet we all accomplish them every night. In a subjective sense—and Poe's thought is wholly subjective—we destroy the world every time we close our eyes. If *esse est percipi*, as Bishop Berkeley said—if to be is to be perceived—then when we withdraw our attention from the world in somnolence or sleep, the world ceases to be. As our minds move toward sleep, by way of drowsiness and reverie and the hypnagogic state, we escape from consciousness of the world, we escape from awareness of our bodies, and we enter a realm in which reason no longer hampers the play of the imagination: we enter the realm of dream.

Like many romantic poets, Poe identified imagination with dream. Where Poe differed from other romantic poets was in the literalness and absoluteness of the identification, and in the clinical precision with which he observed the phenomena of dream, carefully distinguishing the various states through which the mind passes on its way to sleep. A large number of Poe's stories derive their very structure from this sequence of mental states: "Ms. Found in a Bottle," to give but one example, is an allegory of the mind's voyage from the waking world into the world of dreams, with each main step of the narrative symbolizing the passage of the mind from one state to another—from wakefulness to reverie, from reverie to the hypnagogic state, from the hypnagogic state to the deep dream. The departure of the narrator's ship from Batavia represents the mind's withdrawal from the waking world; the drowning of the captain and all but one of the crew represents the growing solitude of reverie; when the narrator is transferred by collision from a real ship to a phantom ship, we are to understand that he has passed from reverie, a state in which reality and dream exist in a kind of equilibrium, into the free fantasy of the hypnagogic state. And when the phantom ship makes its final plunge into the whirlpool, we are to understand that the narrator's mind has gone over the brink of sleep and descended into dreams.

What I am saying by means of this example is that the scenes and situations of Poe's tales are always concrete representations of states of mind. If we bear in mind Poe's fundamental plot—the effort of the poetic soul to escape all consciousness of the world in dream—we soon recognize the significance of certain scenic or situational motifs which

turn up in story after story. The most important of these recurrent motifs is that of *enclosure* or *circumscription;* perhaps the latter term is preferable, because it is Poe's own
word, and because Poe's enclosures are so often more or less
circular in form. The heroes of Poe's tales and poems are violently circumscribed by whirlpools, or peacefully circumscribed by cloud-capped Paradisal valleys; they float upon
circular pools ringed in by steep flowering hillsides; they
dwell on islands, or voyage to them; we find Poe's heroes
also in coffins, in the cabs of balloons, or hidden away in the
holds of ships; and above all we find them sitting alone in
the claustral and richly-furnished rooms of remote and
mouldering mansions.

Poe's Motifs of Enclosure

Almost never, if you think about it, is one of Poe's heroes to
be seen standing in the light of common day; almost never
does the Poe hero breathe the air that others breathe; he requires some kind of envelope in order to be what he is; he is
always either enclosed or on his way to an enclosure. The
narrative of William Wilson conducts the hero from Stoke
Newington to Eton, from Eton to Oxford, and then to Rome
by way of Paris, Vienna, Berlin, Moscow, Naples, and Egypt:
and yet, for all his travels, Wilson seems never to set foot out-
of-doors. The story takes place in a series of rooms, the last
one locked from the inside.

Sometimes Poe emphasizes the circumscription of his heroes by multiple enclosures. Roderick Usher dwells in a
great and crumbling mansion from which, as Poe tells us, he
has not ventured forth in many years. This mansion stands
islanded in a stagnant lake, which serves it as a defensive
moat. And beyond the moat lies the Usher estate, a vast barren tract having its own peculiar and forbidding weather
and atmosphere. You might say that Roderick Usher is defended in depth; and yet at the close of the story Poe com-
pounds Roderick's inaccessibility by having the mansion
and its occupant swallowed up by the waters of the tarn.

What does it mean that Poe's heroes are invariably enclosed or circumscribed? The answer is simple: circumscription, in Poe's tales, means the exclusion from consciousness of the so-called real world, the world of time and
reason and physical fact; it means the isolation of the poetic
soul in visionary reverie or trance. When we find one of Poe's

characters in a remote valley, or a claustral room, we know that he is in the process of dreaming his way out of the world.

Now, I want to [consider] one kind of enclosure in Poe's tales: the mouldering mansion and its richly-furnished rooms. I want to concentrate on Poe's architecture and decor for two reasons: first, because Poe's use of architecture is so frankly and provably allegorical that I *should* be able to be convincing about it; second, because by concentrating on one area of Poe's symbolism we shall be able to see that his stories are allegorical not only in their broad patterns, but also in their smallest details.

"THE HAUNTED PALACE"

Let us begin with a familiar poem, "The Haunted Palace." The opening stanzas of this poem, as a number of critics have noted, make a point-by-point comparison between a building and the head of a man. The exterior of the palace represents the man's physical features; the interior represents the man's mind engaged in harmonious imaginative thought.

> In the greenest of our valleys,
>   By good angels tenanted,
> Once a fair and stately palace—
>   Radiant palace—reared its head.
> In the monarch Thought's dominion,
>   It stood there!
> Never seraph spread a pinion
>   Over fabric half so fair!
>
> Banners yellow, glorious, golden,
>   On its roof did float and flow
> (This—all this—was in the olden
>   Time long ago),
> And every gentle air that dallied,
>   In that sweet day,
> Along the ramparts plumed and pallid,
>   A winged odor went away.
>
> Wanderers in that happy valley,
>   Through two luminous windows, saw
> Spirits moving musically
>   To a lute's well-tuned law,
> Round about a throne where, sitting,
>   Porphyrogene,
> In state his glory well befitting,
>   The ruler of the realm was seen.
>
> And all in pearl and ruby glowing
>   Was the fair palace door,

Through which came flowing, flowing, flowing,
    And sparkling evermore,
A troop of Echoes, whose sweet duty
    Was but to sing,
In voices of surpassing beauty,
    The wit and wisdom of their king.

I expect you observed that the two luminous windows of the palace are the eyes of a man, and that the yellow banners on the roof are his luxuriant blond hair. The "pearl and ruby" door is the man's mouth—ruby representing red lips, and pearl representing pearly white teeth. The beautiful Echoes which issue from the pearl and ruby door are the poetic utterances of the man's harmonious imagination, here symbolized as an orderly dance. The angel-guarded valley in which the palace stands, and which Poe describes as "the monarch Thought's dominion," is a symbol of the man's exclusive awareness of exalted and spiritual things. The valley is what Poe elsewhere called "that evergreen and radiant paradise which the true poet knows . . . as the limited realm of his authority, as the circumscribed Eden of his dreams."

The last two stanzas of the poem describe the physical and spiritual corruption of the palace and its domain, and it was to this part of the poem that Poe was referring when he told a correspondent, "By the 'Haunted Palace' I mean to imply a mind haunted by phantoms—a disordered brain." [These are] the closing lines:

But evil things, in robes of sorrow,
    Assailed the monarch's high estate.
(Ah, let us mourn!—for never morrow
    Shall dawn upon him, desolate!)
And round about his home the glory
    That blushed and bloomed,
Is but a dim-remembered story
    Of the old time entombed.

And travellers, now, within that valley,
    Through the red-litten windows see
Vast forms that move fantastically
    To a discordant melody,
While, like a ghastly rapid river,
    Through the pale door
A hideous throng rush out forever,
    And laugh—but smile no more.

The domain of the monarch Thought, in these final stanzas, is disrupted by civil war, and in consequence everything alters for the worse. The valley becomes barren, like the domain of Roderick Usher; the eye-like windows of the palace are no longer "luminous," but have become "red-litten"— they are like the bloodshot eyes of a madman or a drunkard. As for the mouth of our allegorized man, it is now "pale" rather than "pearl and ruby," and through it come no sweet Echoes, as before, but the wild laughter of a jangling and discordant mind.

Two States of Mind

The two states of the palace—before and after—are, as we can see, two states of mind. Poe does not make it altogether clear *why* one state of mind has given way to the other, but by recourse to similar tales and poems we can readily find the answer. The palace in its original condition expresses the imaginative harmony which the poet's soul enjoys in early childhood, when all things are viewed with a tyrannical and unchallenged subjectivity. But as the soul passes from childhood into adult life, its consciousness is more and more invaded by the corrupt and corrupting external world: it succumbs to passion, it develops a conscience, it makes concessions to reason and to objective fact. Consequently, there is civil war in the palace of the mind. The imagination must now struggle against the intellect and the moral sense: finding itself no longer able to possess the world through a serene solipsism, it strives to annihilate the outer world by turning in upon itself; it flees into irrationality and dream; and all its dreams are efforts both to recall and to simulate its primal, unfallen state.

"The Haunted Palace" presents us with a possible key to the general meaning of Poe's architecture; and this key proves, if one tries it, to open every building in Poe's fiction. Roderick Usher, as you will remember, declaims "The Haunted Palace" to the visitor who tells his story, accompanying the poem with wild improvisations on the guitar. We are encouraged, therefore, to compare the palace of the poem with the house of the story; and it is no surprise to find that the Usher mansion has "vacant eye-like windows," and that there are mysterious physical sympathies between Roderick Usher and the house in which he dwells. The House of Usher *is*, in allegorical fact, the physical body of Roderick Usher, and its dim interior *is*, in fact, Roderick Usher's visionary mind.

The House of Usher, like many edifices in Poe, is in a state of extreme decay. The stonework of its facade has so crumbled and decomposed that it reminds the narrator, as he puts it, "of the specious totality of old woodwork which has rotted for long years in some neglected vault." The Usher mansion is so eaten away, so fragile, that it seems a breeze would push it over; it remains standing only because the atmosphere of Usher's domain is perfectly motionless and dead. Such is the case also with the "time-eaten towers that tremble not" in Poe's poem "The City in the Sea"; and likewise the magnificent architecture of "The Domain of Arnheim" is said to "sustain itself by a miracle in mid-air." Even the detective Dupin lives in a perilously decayed structure: the narrator of "The Murders in the Rue Morgue" tells how he and Dupin dwelt in a "time-eaten and grotesque mansion, long deserted through superstitions into which we did not enquire, and tottering to its fall in a retired and desolate portion of the Faubourg St. Germain." (Notice how, even when Poe's buildings are situated in cities, he manages to circumscribe them with a protective desolation.)

We must now ask what Poe means by the extreme and tottering decay of so many of his structures. The answer is best given by reference to "The Fall of the House of Usher," and in giving the answer we shall arrive, I think, at an understanding of the pattern of that story.

A JOURNEY INTO THE SELF

"The Fall of the House of Usher" is a journey into the depths of the self. I have said that all journeys in Poe are allegories of the process of dreaming, and we must understand "The Fall of the House of Usher" as a dream of the narrator's, in which he leaves behind him the waking, physical world and journeys inward toward his *moi intérieur*, toward his inner and spiritual self. That inner and spiritual self is Roderick Usher.

Roderick Usher, then, is a part of the narrator's self, which the narrator reaches by way of reverie. We may think of Usher, if we like, as the narrator's imagination, or as his visionary soul. Or we may think of him as a *state of mind* which the narrator enters at a certain stage of his progress into dreams. Considered as a state of mind, Roderick Usher is an allegorical figure representing the hypnagogic state.

The hypnagogic state, about which there is strangely little said in the literature of psychology, is a condition of semiconsciousness in which the closed eye beholds a continuous procession of vivid and constantly changing forms. These forms sometimes have color, and are often abstract in character. Poe regarded the hypnagogic state as the visionary condition *par excellence*, and he considered its rapidly shifting abstract images to be—as he put it—"glimpses of the spirit's outer world." These visionary glimpses, Poe says in one of his *Marginalia*, "arise in the soul . . . only . . . at those mere points of time where the confines of the waking world blend with those of the world of dreams." And Poe goes on to say: "I am aware of these 'fancies' only when I am upon the very brink of sleep, with the consciousness that I am so."

Roderick Usher enacts the hypnagogic state in a number of ways. For one thing, the narrator describes Roderick's behavior as inconsistent, and characterized by constant alternation: he is alternately vivacious and sullen; he is alternately communicative and rapt; he speaks at one moment with "tremulous indecision," and at the next with the "energetic concision" of an excited opium-eater. His conduct resembles, in other words, that wavering between consciousness and subconsciousness which characterizes the hypnagogic state. The trembling of Roderick's body, and the floating of his silken hair, also bring to mind the instability and underwater quality of hypnagogic images. His improvisations on the guitar suggest hypnagogic experience in their rapidity, changeableness, and wild novelty. And as for Usher's paintings, which the narrator describes as "pure abstractions," they quite simply *are* hypnagogic images. The narrator says of Roderick, "From the paintings over which his elaborate fancy brooded, and which grew, touch by touch, into vaguenesses at which I shuddered the more thrillingly because I shuddered without knowing why—from these paintings (vivid as their images now are before me) I would in vain endeavor to educe more than a small portion which should lie within the compass of merely written words." That the narrator finds Roderick's paintings indescribable is interesting, because in that one of the *Marginalia* from which I have quoted, Poe asserts that the only things in human experience which lie "beyond the compass of words" are the visions of the hypnagogic state.

Roderick Usher stands for the hypnagogic state, which as Poe said is a teetering condition of mind occurring "upon the very brink of sleep." Since Roderick is the embodiment of a state of mind in which *falling*—falling asleep—is imminent, it is appropriate that the building which symbolizes his mind should promise at every moment to fall. The House of Usher stares down broodingly at its reflection in the tarn below, as in the hypnagogic state the conscious mind may stare into the subconscious; the house threatens continually to collapse because it is extremely easy for the mind to slip from the hypnagogic state into the depths of sleep; and when the House of Usher *does* fall, the story ends, as it must, because the mind, at the end of its inward journey, has plunged into the darkness of sleep.

THE SIGNIFICANCE OF DECAY AND DECOMPOSITION

We have found one allegorical meaning in the tottering decay of Poe's buildings; there is another meaning, equally important, which may be stated very briefly. I have said that Poe saw the poet as at war with the material world, and with the material or physical aspects of himself; and I have said that Poe identified poetic imagination with the power to escape from the material and the materialistic, to exclude them from consciousness and so subjectively destroy them. Now, if we recall these things, and recall also that the exteriors of Poe's houses or palaces, with their eye-like windows and mouth-like doors, represent the physical features of Poe's dreaming heroes, then the characteristic dilapidation of Poe's architecture takes on sudden significance. The extreme decay of the House of Usher—a decay so extreme as to approach the atmospheric—is quite simply a sign that the narrator, in reaching that state of mind which he calls Roderick Usher, has very nearly dreamt himself free of his physical body, and of the material world with which that body connects him.

This is what decay or decomposition mean everywhere in Poe; and we find them almost everywhere. Poe's preoccupation with decay is not, as some critics have thought, an indication of necrophilia; decay in Poe is a symbol of visionary remoteness from the physical, a sign that the state of mind represented is one of almost pure spirituality. When the House of Usher disintegrates or dematerializes at the close of the story, it does so because Roderick Usher has become all soul. "The Fall of the House of Usher," then, is not really a horror story; it is a triumphant report by the narrator that it *is* possible for the poetic soul to shake off this temporal, rational, physical world and escape, if only for a moment, to a realm of unfettered vision.

Hawthorne's Use of Allegory

Michael Davitt Bell

Literary critic Michael Davitt Bell is the author of *Hawthorne and the Historical Romance of New England, The Problem of American Realism: Studies in the Cultural History of a Literary Idea,* and *The Development of American Romance: The Sacrifice of Relation,* from which the subsequent selection is excerpted. In this excerpt he contends that while Hawthorne's writing contains allegorical elements, it does not fulfill allegory's goal of illustrating a truth about the world.

In 1852, E.P. Whipple wrote, in a review of *The Blithedale Romance:* "The characters are not really valuable for what they are, but for what they illustrate." In this phrase he put his finger on what is most essentially allegorical about Nathaniel Hawthorne. Allegory is normally associated with didacticism, but it seems wise, for the moment, to defer the whole question of allegorical *intention.* What matters about allegory *as a mode* is that it is illustrative rather than realistically representational. As a mode of expression it is, as Samuel Taylor Coleridge puts it, a "translation of abstract notions into a picture-language." The term "allegory," to rehearse the familiar, derives from Greek roots meaning "to speak other than openly." "In the simplest terms," as Angus Fletcher writes, "allegory says one thing and means another." What allegory "says" in not unimportant; it may have a high degree of realistic content. "The whole point of allegory," according to Fletcher, "is that it does not *need* to be read exegetically; it often has a literal level that makes good enough sense all by itself." Hawthorne, for instance, praised *Pilgrim's Progress* for "the human interest with which the author has so strongly imbued the shadowy beings of his allegory." But such inter-

Excerpted from Michael Davitt Bell, *The Development of American Romance: The Sacrifice of Relation* (Chicago: University of Chicago Press). ©1980 by The University of Chicago. All rights reserved. Reprinted with permission from the publisher.

est, whatever its importance in particular allegories, is not what is "allegorical" about them, for that lies in what we might call their apparent "other-meaningness"—in their seeming to point to "abstract notions" behind their "picture language." Thus Hawthorne characteristically distinguished allegory, at least his own allegories, from the realistic fictions he always claimed to prefer.

In this light, the crucial point about allegory, as an illustrative *mode*, is that it represents reality not immediately but at one remove. In theory, at least, the elements of a realistic fiction—characters, say, or scenes—correspond directly with things in the "real" world—people, say, or places. In an allegorical fiction, by contrast, the correspondence or relation is indirect: the elements represent not things but ideas about things, "abstract notions." These elements may be fleshed out for "human interest," but the essential *relation* in allegory is nevertheless nonrepresentational, intellectual, abstract, illustrative.

THE PARADOX OF HAWTHORNE'S ALLEGORY

For the most part, Hawthorne's practice would appear to fall within these criteria, at least with respect to the *mode* of his fiction. His tales are full of apparently allegorical characters, settings, and, especially, objects: Dr. Rappaccinni, his garden, the Maypole of Merry-Mount, Parson Hooper's black veil, Georgiana's birthmark, the scarlet letter. All of these seem insistently illustrative. In *The Scarlet Letter* we are told of the Beadle, in the opening ceremony, that he "prefigured and represented in his aspect the whole dismal severity of the Puritanic code of law" and, of the scaffold, that "the very ideal of ignominy was embodied and made manifest in this contrivance of wood and iron." These things, in E.P. Whipple's phrase, matter not for what they are, clearly, but for what they illustrate.

The problem, though, is that, while the *mode* of Hawthorne's tales is clearly allegorical, their *intention* is much less clearly so. The author of *The Scarlet Letter* hardly wishes to enforce upon us, as didactic imperatives, either the "dismal severity of the Puritanic code of law" or even "the very ideal of ignominy." These, to quote Coleridge, are the abstract notions for which the Beadle and the scaffold provide the "picture-language." Yet they are not Hawthorne's notions but those of the society about which he is writing. The Beadle and the scaffold, as narrative elements, are allegorical, but they are allegory observed, not allegory imagined. Moreover, what is true of them is generally true in Hawthorne, at least in Hawthorne at his best. His plots are not didactically generated by his efforts to tell us what the symbols mean, what abstract notions they picture forth; they grow instead out of his characters' efforts to find out what the symbols mean or at all events to make them mean something. It is these characters who are, in intention, the allegorists. Moreover, their allegorical tendency almost always leads to a distortion of life, a refusal to face it directly in its full complexity. Hawthorne thus apparently adopts the allegorical mode in order to turn it against allegorical intentions.

ALLEGORY IN "YOUNG GOODMAN BROWN"

This paradoxical aspect of Hawthorne's allegory can be seen in what is probably his best-known tale. "Young Goodman Brown" can be taken as a realistic story of a young man of late seventeenth-century Salem, turned to bitterness by a real or imaginary visit to a witches' sabbath in the woods. This is the story's "human interest," and, as several readers have ably demonstrated, this interest is firmly rooted in actual seventeenth-century New England history. Still, the story's *mode* of dealing with historical reality is not realistic but allegorical. The action is presented without overt attention to motive or causality. The imagery is iconographically evocative rather than verisimilar. The old man whom Brown meets in the woods is less a realized character than the illustration of and spokesman for an idea: the university of sin. Brown's wife is scarcely characterized or even described; she exists simply as a compound of two illustrative details—her pink ribbons and her archly suggestive name, "Faith." Finally, the witches' nocturnal sabbath, for all its lurid detail, is also primarily allegorical, illustrative of the devil's statement, which comes at its climax: "Evil is the nature of mankind."

If the elements of "Young Goodman Brown" thus seem to serve an illustrative function, this function can hardly be didactic; for while the characters and settings represent ideas, they are Brown's ideas, not Hawthorne's. The old man, for example, isn't so much an allegorical devil—Hawthorne's symbol of abstract evil—as he is a projection either of Brown's own growing knowledge of evil or of his unacknowledged impulse toward it. Even the witches' sabbath may be, as its abrupt termination strongly suggests, Brown's own neurotic hallucination. Several critics have discussed the importance of hallucination and projection in "Young Goodman Brown," finding at the center of the tale not a moral—authority figures are "evil"—but a struggle between Brown's conscious reverence for figures of authority and his unconscious impulse to discredit them by imputing to them his own "sinful" urges. We should pay special attention to what such readings suggest about the status of allegorical intention in Hawthorne's allegories. The story's elements do illustrate aspects of Brown's internal psychological conflict, and in this they are perfectly conventional (as in the temptation of Spenser's Redcross by Giant Despayre). What is not conventional is that in "Young Goodman Brown" the illustrative or allegorical *quality* of the symbols is symptomatic of Brown's psychological condition. He is torn between two rigidly "allegorical" possibilities: either humankind is

THE FUNCTION OF ALLEGORY IN *THE SCARLET LETTER*

Hawthorne tends in his allegorical narratives to place in close juxtaposition many individual interpretations in order to undermine the practical validity of subjective approaches to objective truth. This is certainly the case in *The Scarlet Letter* where the significance of the badge that Hester is condemned to wear refuses to remain static. In Reverend Wilson's sermon, the scarlet letter assumes infernal hues, and yet to a 'papist' the sight of Hester and her child is reminiscent of the Madonna. The narrative creates a figurative link between the scarlet letter and the wild rosebush that grows at the prison door but the narrator steadfastly refuses to create of either, or the narrative itself, 'some sweet moral blossom'. The role of moral arbiter is taken up by the Puritan women, whose responses to Hester's release from prison are recorded in the following chapter. These moralizations are sharply juxtaposed and represent no consensus of opinion. Rather, they represent the variety of self-interests and egotistical foible to which flesh is heir and which motivate purely personal and subjective interpretations of human behaviour: motivations like envy, jealousy, cruelty, spite, and so on. . . .

All of the characters interpret allegorically, yet these interpretations are not brought to any authoritative synthesis; they remain trenchantly subjective and individual. Hester inter-

"good" or it is "evil"; no other *kind* of meaning is possible for him. Abstract notions here, such as "good" and "evil," are not meanings but essential ingredients in a dramatic situation. "Evil is the nature of mankind" is the devil's meaning, a projection of Brown's self-conscious purity, a notion he finally comes to accept consciously as *his* meaning. What the story is "about" is not the meaning but the acceptance. Brown accepts abstract, allegorical meaning as a displacement for unacknowledgeable impulses—as a refuge from more personal insight.

Hawthorne is a peculiarly aloof sort of allegorist, concerned not with what reality means but with the ways his characters attribute meaning to reality or impose meaning on it. It is his characters who turn life into a picture language by making it illustrate ideas about life, as Brown must make Faith either "good" or "evil." It is in this sense that Brown is an allegorist. And so are many of Hawthorne's characters. What is the much-discussed "Unpardonable Sin," after all,

prets the scarlet letter figuratively: beyond the primary significance of sin she perceives a meaning that offers her a special dispensation from the norms of her society. Alienated from the Puritan community, she rejects its laws and assumes a 'freedom of speculation' that allows her to rethink the entire structure of culturally determined meanings. The 'natural consecration' of her sin that she sees symbolized by her embellishment of the scarlet letter permits her to reconcile the natural with the divine in her vision of the future. Chillingworth, in contrast, concentrates his hermeneutic energies in the search for Hester's co-Adulterer, signified by the scarlet 'A'. Chillingworth seeks the partner in sin who would complete the significance of the letter but a fixed meaning, even such a literal meaning as this, eludes the physician's hermeneutic grasp. For the meaning of the scarlet letter is ambiguously related to a further and even more elusive sign: the living stigmata upon Dimmesdale's breast. The Reverend Dimmesdale is himself caught amid the various significances of the scarlet letter. Divine judgement, carnal sin, paternal guilt: he attempts to bring these meanings together while eluding civil judgement. As a result of his obsession with the physical letter, he never discovers within the sign the spirit that heals; he finds only that the letter can, indeed, kill.

Deborah L. Madsen, *Allegory in America: From Puritanism to Postmodernism*, 1996.

but a kind of allegorical inclination to substitute illustrative meaning for true, realistic sympathy or self-knowledge? So Ethan Brand succumbs to "the Idea that possessed his life," and it is thus that Young Goodman Brown, like most of Hawthorne's Puritans, ends up being trapped by an allegory of his own making. Indeed, the besetting sin of Hawthorne's Puritans—and the one he most frequently scrutinizes, particularly in dealing with the second and third generations—is their insistence on allegorizing experience into rigid "iron" forms, cut off from life and suppressive of it. Through its anti-allegorical manipulation of the allegorical mode, "Young Goodman Brown" illustrates this allegorical tendency in its historical subject. "Evil" may or may not be the "nature of mankind," but there is no doubt, as the final sentence declares of Brown, that "his dying hour was gloom."

Symbolism in *Moby-Dick*

F.O. Matthiessen

F.O. Matthiessen, a well-known literary critic, was the first to use the term "American Renaissance" in reference to American Romanticism. He is the author of a number of books on nineteenth- and twentieth-century American literature. In the following excerpt, taken from his book *American Renaissance: Art and Expression in the Age of Emerson and Whitman,* Matthiessen describes how symbolism operates in Herman Melville's *Moby-Dick.*

The symbols in *Moby-Dick* . . . come with the freshness of a new resource, just as, in spite of its great length, the book is the most compact expression of Herman Melville's enormous imaginative range. In this latter respect a parallel holds with *The Scarlet Letter.* . . .

[Nathaniel Hawthorne] spoke with more emotion of *The Scarlet Letter* than he ever did of any of his other books. He wrote . . . : 'It is . . . positively a hell-fired story, into which I found it almost impossible to throw any cheering light.' It makes a very striking coincidence that Melville, in the midst of the final chapters of *Moby-Dick,* was to use almost the same phrase in writing to Hawthorne about 'the hell-fire in which the whole book is broiled.'

Both works justify the intensity of these phrases, since the chief use for which their symbolical correspondences were designed was to make a searching expression of the tragic dilemmas of the soul. Melville developed his basic contrasts between land and sea, and between calm and storm, both for their own dramatic force, and as his most powerful means of projecting man's inner struggle. The theme of the sea is preluded in the opening pages where Ishmael gives among his reasons for going whaling that 'meditation and water are wedded forever'; and then adds that the tormenting image of himself, which man sees even in fountains and rivers, 'is the image of the ungraspable phantom of life; and this is the key to it all.' That serves to explain in a flash why Melville could find so much in Hawthorne's 'Monsieur du Miroir,' for there also baffled self-scrutiny used the image of Narcissus.

SYMBOLS OF SEA AND LAND

The sea conveys primarily gigantic restless power and obscurity. It is thus placed in opposition to 'the blessed light of the evangelical land'; or, handled humorously, to the tug earthward of New Bedford and Salem, 'where they tell me the young girls breathe such musk, their sailor sweethearts smell them miles off shore, as though they were drawing nigh the odorous Moluccas instead of the Puritanic sands.' No wonder that this fundamental contrast gives Melville the very terms that he needs when, at the moment of the whaler's setting sail on its interminable voyage round the world, he wants to suggest also his kind of voyage, wherein 'all deep, earnest thinking is but the intrepid effort of the soul to keep the open independence of her sea; while the wildest winds of heaven and earth conspire to cast her on the treacherous, slavish shore.'

Midway through the book, when the ship has already reached the whale grounds, a whole chapter is built out of the conflict between these two elements, as a means of forecasting the climax, which both outer and inner worlds are moving towards inexorably. Employing to the full the rhetorical device of parallel iteration, Melville dwells on the aboriginal terrors of the ocean, which no veneer of civilization can gloss over to perceptive eyes. He stresses the elementary fact that no inhabitants of the sea have even the kindness of the dog, but that their very touch has always been repellent to human kind. He shifts the ground to society's furthest development, and declares that 'however baby man may brag of his science and skill, and however much, in a flattering future, that science and skill may augment; yet forever and forever, to the crack of doom, the sea will insult and murder him, and pulverise the stateliest, stiffest frigate he can make.' He asks the reader to consider the subtleness of the sea, how it masks its hidden perils beneath the loveliest azure; to consider its universal cannibalism, since its creatures have been preying on each other, carrying on continual war ever since the world began. 'Consider all this; and then turn to this green, gentle, and most docile earth; consider them both, the sea and the land; and do you not find a strange analogy to something in yourself? For as this appalling ocean surrounds the verdant land, so in the soul of man there lies one insular Tahiti, full of peace and joy, but encompassed by all the horrors of the half-known life. God keep thee! Push not off from that isle, thou canst never return!'

THE PROBLEM OF INTERPRETING SYMBOLS

The problem that has been encountered in the preceding paragraphs, the virtual impossibility of conveying the complex applications of Melville's symbols except in their own words, is posed by the properties of the symbol itself. In discriminating between the truth of science and that of poetry and religion, [literary critic] Austin Warren has said that the abstractions of the former 'give a clearer but thinner knowledge, knowledge *about* reality; reality in itself is never known save through symbols, and the thing symbolized can never, finally, be separated from its vehicle.' That does not mean that there are not differing degrees of truth in what is expressed in symbols, and that a partial vitiation of Melville's analogies may not lie in his romantically idyllic view of the land. But no imaginative symbol can be judged out of its context, and it must be remembered that this contrast between the terms of peace and violence is being made from a deck in mid-ocean by a young man on his first whaling voyage. In addition, Melville partially protects himself by the selection of his 'insular Tahiti,' a primitive state of innocence in which developing mankind may not remain, as Melville knew even when he half envied it in *Typee,* and as he was to express with devastating thoroughness when he came, in *Pierre,* to examine actual life on land.

His richly varying contrasts between calm and storm are less open to any objections. On one level they are part of his dramatic equipment, for from the first lowering to the final three days' chase, the great actions of his tragedy are invariably made to spring from a quiet sea, as if to heighten the ferocity of Ahab's relentless pursuit. As another facet of Melville's effect, the calmness of the Pacific finds its way into the slow rise and fall of some of his most remarkably sustained prose rhythms; for hardly less than James Joyce's pages on the Liffey does Melville's pattern of language become one with the flux and sound of what it describes. That, to be sure, is a short-hand account of the process, suggested by Ralph Waldo Emerson's terminology, for Melville's rare ability to convey a sense of the movement of the sea depends not on literal imitation, which would be impossible, but rather on his discovery that all rhythm has a physical basis, on his own intimate response to the rhythm of the sea, and on his skill in re-creating his impression in words.

But the full meaning of the sea was not exhausted for Melville in the way its long-breathed undulations could give rise to his own tranquil, almost dreamlike thoughts. As Melville construes it, calm is but the fragile envelope of storm; it is mere delusive appearance, like the treacherous repose of Moby-Dick himself, for the truth is violent and tempestuous. Sometimes Melville varies his interpretation, as in 'The Grand Armada,' where he describes the formation of a vast herd of whales, which arranged itself in a circle of two or three miles, thus making a protected region for the mothers and young. Ishmael had seen it all, since, to his terror, the boat in which he was one of the crew was dragged by a harpooned whale to the very center of this circle. There, as the whale finally broke loose, they glided as on the bosom of a lake, though surrounded on all sides by ominously heaving forms. Ishmael suddenly reflected that 'even so, amid the tornadoed Atlantic of my being, do I myself still forever centrally disport in mute calm; and while ponderous planets of unwaning woe revolve round me, deep down and deep inland there I still bathe me in eternal mildness of joy.'

But even this masterly self-reliance, as Melville knows, is liable to be swept by forces far beyond its control, just as the whole shipful of men, bathed in the tranquillity of sunset, plunges ahead into the dark of Ahab's tyrannic will. This force is symbolized in another remarkable chapter, 'The Try-Works,' where the act of burning down the blubber on the ship's deck at night becomes, in its lurid flame, 'the material counterpart of her monomaniac commander's soul.' It seemed then to Ishmael, in a rare symbol for individualistic recklessness—indeed for a whole era of American development—'that whatever swift, rushing thing I stood on was not so much bound to any haven ahead as rushing from all havens astern.'

HOW SYMBOLS OPERATE IN *MOBY-DICK*

The fact that Melville's most effective symbols expand thus from indicated analogies into the closely wrought experience of whole chapters, and that such a quality as whiteness can hold different contents at different times, or indeed at the same time, should emphasize the futility of the game which was so popular a decade ago, of trying to 'spot' in a paragraph exactly what the white whale stands for. To D.H. Lawrence, we remember, it was 'the last phallic being of the white man,' its blood-consciousness sought out for destruction by the thin intellect. [Literary critic] Van Wyck Brooks was reminded of the monster Grendel in *Beowulf*, another record in the Northern consciousness of the hard fight against the savage elements. To the disciple of psychiatrist Carl Jung, said [literary critic] Lewis Mumford, it could stand for the Unconscious itself, which torments man, and is yet the source of all his boldest efforts. There is no lack of critical challenge in these suggestions, and in so far as they stress Melville's penetration to the primitive forces of experience, to the element of the irrational, they possess a basic relevance to the book. But the only way to convey the intricate significances of the white whale would be to quote the two entire chapters wherein, after the ship has been some weeks at sea and Ahab has announced the real purpose of his voyage, this great phenomenon is described.

Melville's sequence here is noteworthy. He devotes the first of these chapters, 'Moby-Dick,' to making his readers suspend disbelief in the circumstantial account of this whale's unexampled, intelligent malignity, by emphasizing how the whalemen's own superstitions go much further in accepting him as ubiquitous, if not immortal. It is only when he has thus planted in our consciousness this mixture of professed observation, which shades off into folklore, that he risks developing his philosophical meditation on 'The Whiteness of the Whale.' This chapter brings us to another of his central themes, that despite the conventional pure and mild connotations of heavenly radiance, there is terror at the heart of worship—a theme which is underscored by his continual contrast between calm and storm. But thus to state the theme of this chapter is no more to give the meaning of the white whale than a paraphrase of the content of a poem reproduces your experience of it. A created symbol, in contrast with allegory, is dynamic; 'its components, not to be equated with anything else, function in their own right.' It is 'a total communication,' in which thought and feeling have become one. This is not, of course, to deny that, just as you appreci-

ate a poem line by line as well as in its cumulative impression, you can also experience Melville's amazing union of
opposites, the fleece of innocence with ferocity, in a single
sentence that almost blinds you with its excess of whiteness:
'Judge, then, to what pitches of inflamed distracted fury the
minds of his more desperate hunters were impelled, when
amid the chips of chewed boats, and the sinking limbs of
torn comrades, they swam out of the white curds of the
whale's direful wrath into the serene exasperating sunlight,
that smiled on, as if at a birth or a bridal.'

The Symbols in Whitman's "When Lilacs Last in the Dooryard Bloom'd"

Charles Feidelson Jr.

Charles Feidelson Jr. is the editor of two anthologies of literary criticism: *Interpretations of American Literature* and *The Modern Tradition: Backgrounds of Modern Literature.* He is also the author of *Symbolism in American Literature*, from which the following selection is excerpted. In this selection, Feidelson suggests that Walt Whitman's poem "When Lilacs Last in the Dooryard Bloom'd" is a symbolic representation of the act of writing the poem itself.

"This subject of language," Walt Whitman confided to [biographer] Horace Traubel, "interests me—interests me: I never quite get it out of my mind. I sometimes think the Leaves is only a language experiment." *An American Primer*, Whitman's fragmentary lecture on language, reveals a mind that fed upon words: "*Names* are magic.—One word can pour such a flood through the soul." The sense of language as inherently significant is his meeting ground with Nathaniel Hawthorne, for whom a "deep meaning . . . streamed forth" from the scarlet letter. In both cases attention is deflected from "ideas" and "objects" to a symbolic medium; and in both cases the perception of a meaningful symbol is opposed to another kind of perception, which Hawthorne calls "analysis." Hawthorne would like to reduce the meaning to the rational terms of logical construct or empirical fact; he is plainly uncomfortable at the disturbance of his "sensibilities." In practice, he not only translates symbolism into allegory but also affects a rational style which ties his language down to the common-sense world. Whitman's awareness of words in themselves is stronger, and he is militantly hostile to reason. He proposes "new law-forces of spoken and written language—not merely the pedagogue-forms, correct, regular, familiar with precedents, made for matters of outside propriety, fine words, thoughts definitely told out." He is indifferent to dictionary words and textbook grammar, which he associates with a barren formalism and externality. Fully accepting the intuition at which Hawthorne boggled, he takes his departure from a denial of conventional distinctions: "Strange and hard that paradox true I give, / Objects gross and the unseen soul are one." Since Whitman regards meaning as an activity of words rather than an external significance attached to them, language, together with the self and the material world, turns out to be a process, the pouring of the flood. "A perfect user of words uses things," while at the same time he *is* both the words and the things:

> Latent, in a great user of words, must actually be all passions, crimes, trades, animals, stars, God, sex, the past, might, space, metals and the like—because these are the words, and he who is not these plays with a foreign tongue, turning helplessly to dictionaries and authorities.

This kind of speech "seldomer tells a thing than suggests or necessitates it," because to "tell" something would be to suppose something outside the language. The reader is not given statements but is set in action, "on the assumption that the process of reading is not a half-sleep, but, in highest sense, an exercise, a gymnast's struggle." The poem necessarily works "by curious removes, indirections," rather than direct imitation of nature, since "the image-making faculty" runs counter to the habit of mind which views the material world as separable from ideas and speech. Whitman's running battle with the rational assumptions of conventional thought reaches its peak in the hyperbolical "Song of the Rolling Earth," where he identifies all "audible words" with the marks on the printed page and glorifies, by way of contrast, "the unspoken meanings of the earth." In deliberate paradox he asserts that true poems will somehow be made from these inaudible words. The poem expresses the bravado of his conscious attempt to create a wholly symbolic language in the face of intellectual convention. For that is his purpose: the "tallying" of things and man, to which he often alludes mysteriously, is simply the presence of language in each and the presence of each in language. The "language experiment" of *Leaves of Grass*—its promise of "new potentialities of speech"—depends on the symbolic status claimed by the book as a whole and in every part. "From the eyesight proceeds another eyesight and from the hearing proceeds another hearing and from the voice proceeds another voice eternally curious of the harmony of things with man."

"WHEN LILACS LAST IN THE DOORYARD BLOOM'D"

The patent symbols of Whitman's best poem, "When Lilacs Last in the Dooryard Bloom'd," are conditioned by the thoroughgoing symbolism of his poetic attitude. As in most elegies, the person mourned is hardly more than the occasion of the work; but this poem, unlike *Lycidas* or *Adonais*, does not transmute the central figure merely by generalizing him out of all recognition. Lincoln is seldom mentioned either as a person or as a type. Instead, the focus of the poem is a presentation of the poet's mind at work in the context of Lincoln's death. If the true subject of *Lycidas* and *Adonais* is not Edward King or John Keats but the Poet, the true subject of Whitman's "Lilacs" is not the Poet but the poetic process. And even this subject is not treated simply by generalizing a particular situation. The act of poetizing and the context in which it takes place have continuity in time and space by no particular existence. Both are "ever-returning"; the tenses shift; the poet is in different places at once; and at the end this whole phase of creation is moving inexorably forward.

THE ACHIEVEMENT OF A POETIC UTTERANCE

Within this framework the symbols behave like characters in a drama, the plot of which is the achievement of a poetic utterance. The spring, the constant process of rebirth, is threaded by the journey of the coffin, the constant process of death, and in the first section it presents the poet with twin symbols: the perennially blooming lilac and the drooping star. The spring also brings to the poet the "thought of him I love," in which the duality of life and death is repeated. The thought of the dead merges with the fallen star in Section 2; the thought of love merges with the life of the lilac, from which the poet breaks a sprig in Section 3. Thus the lilac and the star enter the poem not as objects to which the poet assigns a meaning but as elements in the undifferentiated stream of thoughts and things; and the spring, the real process of becoming, which involves the real process of dissolution, is also the genesis of poetic vision. The complete pattern of the poem is established with the advent of the bird in the fourth section. For here, in the song of the thrush, the lilac and star are united (the bird sings "death's outlet song of life"), and the potentiality of the poet's "thought" is intimated. The song of the bird and the thought of the poet, which also unites life and death, both lay claim to the third place in the "trinity" brought by spring; they are, as it were, the actuality and the possibility of poetic utterance, which reconciles opposite appearances.

The drama of the poem will be a movement from possible to actual poetic speech, as represented by the "tallying" of the songs of the poet and the thrush. Although it is a movement without steps, the whole being implicit in every moment, there is a graduation of emphasis. Ostensibly, the visions of the coffin and the star (Sections 5 through 8) delay the unison of poet and bird, so that full actualization is reserved for the end of the poem. On the other hand, the verse that renders the apparition of the coffin *is* "death's outlet song of life." The poetic act of evoking the dark journey is treated as the showering of death with lilac:

> Here, coffin that slowly passes,
> I give you my sprig of lilac. . . .
> Blossoms and branches green to coffins all I bring,
> For fresh as the morning, thus would I chant a song for you,
>   O sane and sacred death.

Even as the poet lingers, he has attained his end. And the star of Section 8, the counterpart of the coffin, functions in much the same way. The episode that occurred "a month since"—when "my soul in its trouble dissatisfied sank, as where you sad orb, / Concluded, dropt in the night, and was gone"—was a failure of the poetic spring. The soul was united with the star but not with the lilac. Yet the passage is preceded by the triumphant statement, "Now I know what you must have meant," and knowledge issues in the ability to render the episode in verse. The perception of meaning gives life to the fact of death; the star meant the death of Lincoln, but the evolution of the meaning is poetry.

The recurrence of the song of the thrush in the following section and in Section 13 is a reminder of the poetic principle which underlies the entire poem. In a sense, the words, "I hear your notes, I hear your call," apply to all that precedes and all that is to come, for the whole poem, existing in an eternal present, is the "loud human song" of the poet's "brother." But again Whitman delays the consummation. He is "detained" from his rendezvous with the bird although he really "hears" and "understands" all the time by the sight of the "lustrous star" and by the "mastering odor" of the lilac. Since both the star and the lilac are inherent in the song of the bird, he actually lingers only in order to proceed. While the song rings in the background, the poet puts the questions presupposed by his own poetizing. How can the life of song be one with the fact of death?—"O how shall I warble myself for the dead one there I loved?" And what will be the content of the song of death?—"O what shall I hang on the chamber walls . . . / To adorn the burial-house of him I love?" The questions answer themselves. The breath by which the grave becomes part of his chant is the breath of life; within the poem the image of the "burial-house" will be overlaid with "pictures of growing spring." The delay has served only to renew the initial theme: the poet's chant, like the song of the thrush, is itself the genesis of life and therefore contains both life and death.

The final achievement of poetic utterance comes in Section 14, when the poet, looking forth on the rapid motion of life, experiences death. More exactly, he walks between the "thought" and the "knowledge" of death, which move beside him like companions. Just as his poem exists between the "thought" of the dead, which is paradoxically an act of life, and the actual knowledge of the bird's song, which embodies both dying star and living lilac, the poet himself is in motion from the potential to the actual. From this point to the end of the poem, the sense of movement never flags. The poet's flight into the darkness is a fusion with the stream of music from the bird:

> And the charm of the carol rapt me,
> As I held as if by their hands my comrades in the night,
> And the voice of my spirit tallied the song of the bird.

As the motion of the poet is lost in the motion of the song, the latter is identified with the "dark mother always gliding near," and in the "floating" carol death itself becomes the movement of waves that "undulate round the world." In effect, poet and bird, poem and song, life and death, are now the sheer process of the carol; as in "Out of the Cradle Endlessly Rocking," reality is the unfolding Word. The presented song merges into the "long panoramas of visions" in Section 15, and then the inexorable process begins to leave this moment behind:

> Passing the visions, passing the night,
> Passing, unloosing the hold of my comrades' hands,
> Passing the song of the hermit bird and the tallying song
>   of my soul. . . .
> Passing, I leave thee lilac with heart-shaped leaves, . . .
> I cease from my song for thee, . . .
> O comrade lustrous with silver face in the night.

But the poetic activity is continuous; the passing-onward is not a rejection of the old symbols. "Lilac and star and bird twined with the chant of . . . [the] soul" also pass onward because they are activities and not finite things. The conclusion of this poem dramatizes what Whitman once stated of *Leaves of Grass* as a whole—that the book exists as "a passage way to something rather than a thing in itself concluded." Taken seriously, in the sense in which there *can* be no "thing in itself concluded," this notion is not, as Whitman sometimes pretended, a mere excuse for haphazard technique but the rationale of a symbolistic method.

CHRONOLOGY

1803

Birth of Ralph Waldo Emerson (d. 1882)

1804

Birth of Nathaniel Hawthorne (d. 1864)

1809

Birth of Edgar Allan Poe (d. 1849)

1810

Birth of Sarah Margaret Fuller (d. 1850)

1817

Birth of Henry David Thoreau (d. 1862)

1819

Birth of Herman Melville (d. 1891); birth of Walt Whitman (d. 1892)

1824

John Quincy Adams is elected president

1828

Hawthorne's *Fanshawe* is published; Andrew Jackson defeats John Quincy Adams in presidential election

1837

Major financial panic in the United States; Hawthorne's *Twice-Told Tales* is published; Emerson's "The American Scholar" is published

1838

John Greenleaf Whittier's *Ballads and Anti-Slavery Poems* is published; Emerson's "The Divinity School Address" is published; Poe's *The Narrative of Arthur Gordon Pym* is published

1839

Their goal to end slavery, moderate abolitionists form the Liberty party

1840

Poe's *Tales of the Grotesque and Arabesque* is published; *The Dial*, a Transcendentalist magazine edited by Emerson and Fuller, begins publication; William Henry Harrison defeats Martin Van Buren in the presidential election

1841

Emerson's *Essays, First Series* is published; Poe's "Murders in the Rue Morgue" is published; George Ripley establishes the utopian community of Brook Farm in Massachusetts; Harrison is inaugurated; at Harrison's untimely death, John Tyler becomes president

1842

Poe's "The Masque of the Red Death" is published; Hawthorne's *Twice-Told Tales* (enlarged edition) is published

1843

Poe's "The Gold-Bug" and "The Black Cat" are published

1844

Emerson's *Essays, Second Series* is published; Fuller's *Summer on the Lakes* is published; *The Dial* ceases publication; James K. Polk defeats Henry Clay in the presidential election

1845

Poe's *The Raven and Other Poems* is published; Fuller's *Woman in the Nineteenth Century* is published; Thoreau begins his two-year residence in the woods near Walden Pond; U.S. annexes Texas territory

1846

U.S. fights and wins a war against Mexico; Hawthorne's *Mosses from an Old Manse* is published; Melville's *Typee* is published; Emerson's *Poems* is published; Poe's "The Cask of Amontillado" and "The Philosophy of Composition" are published; the Wilmot Proviso prohibits the extension of slavery into territories gained from Mexico

1847

Melville's *Omoo* is published; Ripley's Brook Farm disbands

1848

Poe's *Eureka*, "Annabel Lee," "The Bells," and "Eldorado" are published; Thoreau's *A Week on the Concord and Merrimack Rivers* and "Civil Disobedience" are published; Seneca Falls Convention for Women's Rights; Zachary Taylor defeats Lewis Cass and Martin Van Buren in the presidential election

1849

Melville's *Mardi* and *Redburn* are published

1850

Hawthorne's *The Scarlet Letter* is published; Melville's *White-Jacket* is published; Emerson's *Representative Men* is published; Millard Fillmore becomes president

1851

Hawthorne's *The House of the Seven Gables* and *The Snow-Image* are published; Melville's *Moby-Dick* is published

1852

Hawthorne's *The Blithedale Romance* and *A Wonder Book* are published; Melville's *Pierre, or the Ambiguities* is published; Harriet Beecher Stowe's *Uncle Tom's Cabin* is published; Franklin Pierce is elected president

1853

Hawthorne's *Tanglewood Tales* is published; New York and Chicago linked by railroad

1854

Thoreau's *Walden* is published; founding of Republican party

1855

Whitman's *Leaves of Grass* is published; Melville's *Israel Potter* is published

1856

Melville's *Piazza Tales* is published; Emerson's *English Traits* is published; Whitman's *Leaves of Grass* (second edition) is published; James Buchanan wins the presidential election

1857

Commercial and financial panic in the United States; Melville's *The Confidence-Man* is published

1859

John Brown's raid on Harpers Ferry; Stowe's *The Minister's Wooing* is published

1860

Emerson's *The Conduct of Life* is published; Hawthorne's *The Marble Faun* is published; Whitman's *Leaves of Grass* (third and enlarged edition) is published; South Carolina secedes from the Union

1861

Presidency of Abraham Lincoln; ten more states secede from the Union; firing on Fort Sumter signals the beginning of the Civil War

1865

Whitman's *Drum Taps* is published

1866

Melville's *Battle-Pieces* and *Aspects of War* are published

1924

Billy Budd, Melville's final work, is published posthumously

FOR FURTHER RESEARCH

CRITICISM AND LITERARY
HISTORY ON AMERICAN ROMANTICISM

Quentin Anderson, *Making Americans: An Essay on Individualism and Money.* New York: Harcourt Brace Jovanovich, 1992.

Newton Arvin, *American Pantheon.* New York: Delacorte, 1966.

James Barbour and Thomas Quirk, eds. *Romanticism: Critical Essays in American Literature.* New York: Garland, 1986.

Michael Davitt Bell, *The Development of American Romance: The Sacrifice of Relation.* Chicago: University of Chicago Press, 1980.

Emily Miller Budick, *Fiction and Historical Consciousness: The American Romance Tradition.* New Haven, CT: Yale University Press, 1989.

———, *Nineteenth-Century American Romance: Genre and the Construction of Democratic Culture.* New York: Twayne, 1996.

Kenneth Walter Cameron, *Scholar's Companion to the American Renaissance.* Hartford, CT: Transcendental Books, 1977.

Evan Carton, *The Rhetoric of American Romance: Dialectic and Identity in Emerson, Dickinson, Poe, and Hawthorne.* Baltimore: Johns Hopkins University Press, 1985.

George Dekker, *The American Historical Romance.* New York: Cambridge University Press, 1987.

Edgar A. Dryden, *The Form of the American Romance.* Baltimore: Johns Hopkins University Press, 1998.

Julie Ellison, *Emerson's Romantic Style.* Princeton, NJ:

Princeton University Press, 1984.

Richard Harter Fogle, *The Permanent Pleasure: Essays on Classics of Romanticism.* Athens: University of Georgia Press, 1974.

Henry L. Golemba, *Thoreau's Wild Rhetoric.* New York: New York University Press, 1990.

Russell B. Goodman, *American Philosophy and the Romantic Tradition.* New York: Cambridge University Press, 1990.

Bruce Robert Greenfield, *Narrating Discovery: The Romantic Explorer in American Literature, 1790–1855.* New York: Columbia University Press, 1992.

Michael J. Hoffman, *The Subversive Vision: American Romanticism in Literature.* Port Washington, NY: Kennikat, 1972.

Anne Janowitz, ed., *Romanticism and Gender.* Cambridge, MA: D.S. Brewer, 1998.

Kenneth R. Johnston et al., eds., *Romantic Revolutions: Criticism and Theory.* Bloomington: Indiana University Press, 1990.

Todd M. Lieber, *Endless Experiments: Essays on the Heroic Experience in American Romanticism.* Columbus: Ohio State University Press, 1973.

F.O. Matthiessen, *American Renaissance: Art and Expression in the Age of Emerson and Whitman.* New York: Oxford University Press, 1941.

Tremaine McDowell, ed., *The Romantic Triumph: American Literature from 1830 to 1860.* New York: Macmillan, 1949.

David Morse, *American Romanticism.* Houndsmills, Basingstoke: Macmillan, 1987.

Vernon Louis Parrington, *Main Currents in American Thought.* Vol. 2. *The Romantic Revolution in America.* New York: Harcourt Brace & World, 1927.

Joel Porte, *In Respect to Egotism: Studies in American Romantic Writing.* New York: Cambridge University Press, 1991.

Bernard Rosenthal, *City of Nature: Journeys to Nature in the Age of American Romanticism.* Cranbury, NJ: Associated University Presses, 1980.

Larzer Ziff, *Literary Democracy: The Declaration of Cultural Independence in America.* New York: Viking, 1981.

CRITICISM AND LITERARY HISTORY ON TRANSCENDENTALISM

Catherine L. Albanese, *Corresponding Motion: Transcendental Religion and the New America.* Philadelphia: Temple University Press, 1977.

Paul F. Boller Jr., *American Transcendentalism, 1830–1860: An Intellectual Inquiry.* New York: Putnam, 1974.

Lawrence Buell, *Literary Transcendentalism: Style and Vision in the American Renaissance.* Ithaca, NY: Cornell University Press, 1973.

Richard Francis, *Transcendental Utopias: Individual and Community at Brook Farm, Fruitlands, and Walden.* Ithaca, NY: Cornell University Press, 1997.

Octavius Brooks Frothingham, *Transcendentalism in New England, a History.* New York: Harper, 1959.

Philip F. Gura and Joel Myerson, eds., *Critical Essays on American Transcendentalism.* Boston: G.K. Hall, 1982.

Donald N. Koster, *Transcendentalism in America.* Boston: Twayne, 1975.

Joel Myerson, ed., *Critical Essays on Margaret Fuller.* Boston: G.K. Hall, 1980.

Anne C. Rose, *Transcendentalism as a Social Movement, 1830–1850.* New Haven, CT: Yale University Press, 1981.

Myron Simon and Thornton H. Parsons, eds., *Transcendentalism and Its Legacy.* Ann Arbor: University of Michigan Press, 1966.

George Frisbie Whicher, *The Transcendentalist Revolt Against Materialism.* Boston: Heath, 1965.

HISTORICAL BACKGROUND

Avery Odelle Craven, *Civil War in the Making, 1815–1860.* Baton Rouge: Louisiana State University Press, 1959.

Leo P. Hirrel, *Children of Wrath: New School Calvinism and Antebellum Reform.* Lexington: University Press of Kentucky, 1998.

Lawrence Lader, *The Bold Brahmins: New England's War Against Slavery, 1831–1863.* New York: Dutton, 1961.

Ira M. Leonard and Robert D. Parnet, *American Nativism, 1830–1860.* New York: Van Nostrand Reinhold, 1971.

William Lee Miller, *Arguing About Slavery: The Great Battle in the United States Congress.* New York: Knopf, 1996.

Charles Henry Peck, *The Jacksonian Epoch.* New York: Harper, 1899.

Robert V. Remini, *Andrew Jackson and the Course of American Democracy, 1833–1845.* New York: Harper, 1984.

Martin Ridge and Ray Allen Billington, eds., *America's Frontier Story: A Documentary History of Westward Expansion.* New York: Holt, Rinehart, and Winston, 1969.

John David Smith and Thomas H. Appleton Jr., eds., *A Mythic Land Apart: Reassessing Southerners and Their History.* Westport, CT: Greenwood Press, 1997.

Major L. Wilson, *Space, Time, and Freedom: The Quest for Nationality and the Irrepressible Conflict, 1815–1861.* Westport, CT: Greenwood Press, 1974.

INDEX

abolitionist movement,
American Romanticism's
contribution to, 23–24, 30
Adams, John Quincy, 16
Age of Reason, 39
Ahab (*Moby-Dick*), 41, 122–24
Aids to Reflection (Coleridge),
34
Alcott, Amos Bronson, 19, 28,
60
optimism of, 70–71
allegory
architecture as, in Poe, 137
Hawthorne's use of, 143–48
as illustrative mode, 143–44
nature and human
experience, 46
Amana community, 28
American Pantheon (Arvin),
113
*American Renaissance: Art and
Expression in the Age of
Emerson and Whitman*
(Matthiessen), 149
American Romanticism
humanism of, 44–51
influence of European
Romanticism, 33–34
major themes of, 16
and organic style, 82
split between self and social
role in, 106
unique characteristic of, 57–58
U.S. presidencies during,
27–28
vitality and freshness of, 32
American Romantics

differences in
subjects/literary form
among, 44–45
and external world, tension
between, 85
importance of self-realization
to, 48–50
role of intuition/imagination
for, 50–51
and self-realization, 48–50
sense of human predicament
among, 45–48
and the West, 41–42
"American Scholar, The"
(Emerson), 13, 43, 129
*American Transcendentalism,
1830–1860: An Intellectual
Inquiry* (Boller), 68
An American Primer
(Whitman), 155
Anderson, Quentin, 120
antislavery movement. *See*
abolitionist movement
Anti-Transcendentalists, 23
art
expression of nature in, 81
role of nature in, 76–77
Arvin, Newton, 113
Austen, Jane, 14

"Backward Glance, A"
(Whitman), 115
Barna, Mark Richard, 60
Baudelaire, Charles, 69
Bell, Michael Davitt, 143
Beowulf, 153
Bezanson, Walter E., 36

Billy Budd (Melville), 88
Biographia Literaria
  (Coleridge), 34
"Birth-mark, The"
  (Hawthorne), 14
Blake, William, 14, 34
Blithedale Romance, The
  (Hawthorne), 22–23, 143
Bloomer, Amelia, 31
Boller, Paul F., Jr., 68
Bowers, David, 44
Brook Farm, 21–22, 28
  criticism of, 22–23
Brooks, Cleanth, 20
  on Andrew Jackson, 16
Brooks, Preston (U.S.
  representative), 31
Brooks, Van Wyck, on meaning
  of white whale, 153
Brownson, Orestes, 60, 72
Bryant, William Cullen, 13, 34, 98
  on American vs. European
  landscape, 101
Buell, Lawrence, 75
Burbank, Rex J., 20, 27
Burke, Kenneth, 126
Byron, Lord, 14, 34

Cabot, James Elliot, 100
Call Me Ishmael (Olson), 97
Calvinism, 33
Cameron, Sharon, 94
Canby, Henry Seidel, 62
  on Whitman, 113, 114
capitalism, Whitman's view of,
  117
Carlyle, Thomas, 34, 65, 68
  on optimism of Emerson, 69
Carpenter, Frederick Ives, 19
Carton, Evan, 128
"Celestial Railroad, The"
  (Hawthorne), 68
Channing, Ellery, 64–65
Channing, William Ellery, on
  progress as human destiny,
  60, 65, 73–74
Chateaubriand, 102
"City in the Sea, The" (Poe), 140
*City of Nature: Journeys to
  Nature in the Age of American*

Romanticism (Rosenthal), 84
Civil Disobedience (Thoreau),
  24, 110
  influence of, 107
civilization, as purest form of
  nature, 86
Civil War, as end of American
  Romanticism, 23
Clarel (Melville), 88
Clarke, J.F., 74
Cole, Thomas, 101, 102
Coleridge, Samuel Taylor, 15,
  37, 143
  influence on
    Transcendentalism, 65
  on nature, 99
  on the organic form, 35, 82
  theory of self, 49
Confidence Man, The (Melville),
  54–55, 69, 122
Cooper, James Fenimore, 13, 81
  and transformation of nature,
  86
Cranch, Christopher, 60
Critique of Pure Reason (Kant),
  65
"Cultural Significance of the
  American Wilderness, The"
  (Nash), 79
"Custom House, The"
  (Hawthorne), 14

democracy
  and individualism, conflict
    between, 49
  Jacksonian, 16
Democratic Vistas (Whitman), 57
*Development of American
  Romance: The Sacrifice of
  Relation, The* (Bell), 143
Dial, The (magazine), 18, 19,
  61, 69
  expression of optimism in, 70
Dickens, Charles, 14
Dickinson, Emily, 104
Douglass, Frederick, 23
Dred Scott decision, 31

Edwards, Jonathan, 98
Emerson, Ralph Waldo, 13, 70

anthropocentrism of, 93
on character of the
  Transcendentalists, 18–19
on concept of the Over-Soul,
  20–21
on creative process, 37
development of organic style
  theory, 15
on history, 84–85
humanistic view of, 47
importance of individualism
  to, 40
on Mexican War of 1846, 30
on Napoleon, 41
on need for intuitive thought,
  67
optimism of, 69
patriotism of, 17
as product of native culture, 32
and self-realization, 49, 50
social criticism of, 55–56
on Transcendentalism, 72–73
treatment of evil by, 45
view of nature, 85–86, 99–101
  as mental fabrication, 100
vision of the self, 128–31
enclosure motifs, in Poe,
  133–42
Enlightenment, 58
*Eras and Modes in English
  Poetry* (Miles), 103
"Essay on American Scenery"
  (Cole), 102

"Fall of the House of Usher,
  The" (Poe), 136
  as journey into the self, 140–42
Feidelson, Charles, Jr., 155
Fichte, Johann, 34
Fletcher, Angus, 143
Fogle, Richard Harter, 32
Frankenstein (Shelley), 14
Frost, Robert, 33
Fruitlands (utopian
  community), 28
Frye, Northrop, 87
Fugitive Slave Act, 30, 55
Fuller, Margaret, 19, 31, 70, 75
  on evil, 71
Fulton, Robert, 81

Garrison, William, 30
Gide, André, 69
Gothic literature, 14
government, 39
  force as ultimate foundation
    of, 111–12
  Thoreau on, 108, 109, 110
  as threat to moral integrity,
    108–109

Harrison, W.H., 28
Harvard Divinity School, 65
"Haunted Palace, The" (Poe),
  137–38
Hawthorne, Nathaniel, 41
  concern with human
    isolation, 17
  criticism of Brook Farm,
    22–23
  humanistic view of, 47
  on *Pilgrim's Progress*, 143
  as product of native culture,
    32
  and Puritanism, 53–54
  satire of Transcendentalism
    by, 68
  on *The Scarlet Letter*, 149
  and self-realization, 49–50
  treatment of evil by, 45
  treatment of the regenerative
    quest, 88
  use of allegory by, 143–48,
    155
Hedge, Frederic Henry, 19, 73
Hegel, Georg, 74
Herder, Johann, 34
heroes
  of American Romanticism, 17,
    41
  in Poe, enclosure of, 136
Hester Prynne (*Scarlet Letter*),
  17, 50, 53
"History" (Emerson), 84
Holmes, Oliver Wendell, 32, 33,
  41
Hobbes, Thomas, 34
Hoffman, Michael J., 106
humanism
  in American Romanticism,
    44–51

of Thoreau, 46–47
Hume, David, 20
hypnagogic state, 140
  as Poe's ideal visionary
    condition, 141

idealism, 40, 65–66
imagination
  identification with dream, in
    Poe, 135
  importance in American
    Romanticism, 50–51
  importance to Romanticism, 37
individualism
  and democracy, conflict
    between, 49
  versus egoism/conceit, 37–38
  foundations of, 39–40
  importance to Romanticism,
    37–38
  Thoreau and, 112
  of Whitman, 113–19
industrialization, rise of, 18
Innes, George, 81
introspection, importance in
  American Romanticism, 50–51
Irving, Washington, 13, 81
Ishmael (*Moby-Dick*), 122
  as conception of individual
    existence, 124–26
  as master of reader's
    awareness, 123
  self-reliance of, 152

Jackson, Andrew, 16, 27–28
Jacksonian democracy, 16
James, Henry, Jr., 69
Jefferson, Thomas, 53, 80
Johns, Joshua, 79

"Kansas War" of 1856, 30
Kant, Immanuel, 20, 34, 65
  practical vs. pure reason of, 21
Kaul, A.N., 85
Keats, John, 14
Kennedy, John Pendleton, 41
King, Martin Luther, Jr., 24
Krutch, Joseph Wood, 107

labor movement, rise of, 31

Lackawanna Valley, The
  (Innes), 81
Lanier, Sidney, 32
Lawrence, D.H., on meaning of
  white whale, 153
Leaves of Grass (Whitman), 57,
  89, 157
Lewis, R.W.B., 20
  on Andrew Jackson, 16
Lewis and Clark expedition, 80
Liberator, 30
Lincoln, Abraham, 41
*Literary History of the United
  States* (Bowers), 44
*Literature of the American
  Renaissance, The* (Burbank
  and Moore), 27
Locke, John, 20, 34, 61, 65
"Logic" (Lowell), 30
Longfellow, Henry Wadsworth,
  32, 33
  as abolitionist writer, 30
  and common man, 40
Longstreet, Augustus Baldwin,
  41
Lovejoy, Arthur O., 87
Lowell, James Russell, 30, 32,
  41, 76

Madsen, Deborah L., 15, 147
*Making Americans: An Essay
  on Individualism and Money*
  (Anderson), 120
Manifest Destiny, 17, 64
Marcuse, Herbert, 109
Mardi (Melville), 88, 89, 121
Marx, Karl, 74
Marx, Leo, 81
materialism
  as corrupting influence, 133
  Thoreau on, 111
  Transcendentalists' rejection
    of, 22
Matthiessen, F.O., 32, 82, 149
McDowell, Tremaine, 39
Melville, Herman, 32, 41
  as Anti-Transcendentalist, 23
  conception of individual
    existence, 124–26
  concern with alienation, 18

condemnation of America by, 54–55
humanistic view of, 47
on the new American race, 42
and organicism, 36
satire of Transcendentalism by, 68–69, 122
and self-realization, 49–50
treatment of the regenerative quest, 88
Mexican War of 1846, 30, 55
Miles, Josephine, 103
Milton, John, 57
Moby-Dick (Melville), 24, 54, 69
form of, compared with *The Scarlet Letter*, 36
interaction between characters in, 122
isolation of individual in, 120–27
symbolism in, 149–54
Moore, Jack B., 20, 27
Morley, John, 69
Morse, Samuel F.B., 29
"Ms. Found in a Bottle" (Poe), 135
Mumford, Lewis, on meaning of white whale, 153
"Murders in the Rue Morgue, The" (Poe), 140

Narrative of the Life of an American Slave (Douglass), 23
Nash, Roderick, 79
nationalism
American, rise of, 42–43
political factors affecting, 16
Natural History of Massachusetts (Thoreau), 19
nature
as allegory, 46
Emerson's view of, 85–86
imaginative vision of, 34
as metaphor for regenerative quest, 87–88, 91
as metaphor for the self, 84–91
ending of, 88
Neo-Platonic concept of, 48
role in art, 76–77
role in Transcendentalism, 75–77
as spiritual place, 86–87
Thoreau's view of, 86, 87, 93–94
Transcendentalist's reverence for, 63
Nature (Emerson), 99, 107, 128
anthropocentric view in, 93
as manifesto for Transcendentalism, 62, 87
the self's relation to the world in, 129–30
Negative Romanticism, 107
Neoclassicism, opposition of Romanticism to order of, 81
Neo-Platonism, 62
and concept of nature, 48
New Harmony (utopian community), 28
Newton, Sir Isaac, 34
Nietzsche, Friedrich, 69
Norton, Charles Eliot, 68
novel, American romance, intent of, 14

"Oeconomy of Nature, The" (Linnaeus), 95
Olson, Charles, 97
Omoo (Melville), 120
Oneida community, 28
optimism, 17
differences between American Romantics in, 44
of Emerson, 68–69
in Unitarianism, 20
organicism/organic style
and American Romanticism, 82
in art, 77
description of, 35
philosophy of, 34–38
in poetry, 15
rise of, paralleling sciences, 35
Orphic Sayings (Alcott), 71
O'Toole, Heather, 23
"Out of the Cradle Endlessly Rocking" (Whitman), 159
"Over-Soul, The" (Emerson), 20, 63, 66

nature as manifestation of,
101

parallel iteration, in *Moby-Dick*,
150
Parker, Theodore, 19, 60, 71, 76
Passage to India (Whitman), 29,
87, 88, 89
patriotism, political factors
affecting, 16–17
Peale, Charles Wilson, 80
Pearce, Roy Harvey, 57
Perry, Matthew C., 29
Pierre (Melville), 54, 69, 151
Pilgrim's Progress (Bunyan),
143
Plato, 62, 63
Plotinus, 63
Poe, Edgar Allan, 32
  as Anti-Transcendentalist, 23
  architecture as allegory in,
  137
  decay/decomposition as
  symbols in, 142
  on *The Dial*, 69
  enclosure motifs in, 133–42
  importance of individualism
  to, 40
  influence of European poets
  on, 34
  poetic soul vs. physical world
  in, 134–36
  vision of man and universe,
  52–53
"Poet, The" (Emerson), 98
poetry, Whitman's influence
on, 15
"Poetry and Imagination"
(Emerson), 63
Poirier, Richard, 85
population, U.S., growth in, 29
"Prairies, The" (Bryant), 98
Priestley, Joseph, 80
"Problem, The" (Emerson), 37
progress, Transcendentalist
view of, 71–74
"Progress of Society" (Hedge),
73
Puritanism
  and Hawthorne, 53–54

view on nature, 76
*Purple Mountain Majesty:
Sublime Nature in the U.S.
Capitol* (Johns), 79

railroads, expansion of, 29
reason
  Emerson's meaning of, 62
  practical vs. pure, 21
Redburn (Melville), 121
Reformation, 39
religion, 39
  Christianity,
  Transcendentalist view on,
  76
Renaissance, 39
René (Chateaubriand), 97
"Repressive Tolerance"
(Marcuse), 109
*Rhetoric of American Romance:
Dialectic and Identity in
Emerson, Dickinson, Poe, and
Hawthorne, The* (Carton), 128
Richardson, Robert D., Jr., 63
Ripley, George, 19, 21, 60
  on future of humanity, 71–72
Ripley, Sophia, 21
Roderick Usher, 136, 139
  hypnagogic state of, 140–42
Romanticism
  description of, 34
  European
    influence on American
    Romanticism, 33–34
    view of nature, contrast with
    American view, 97–104
  idealism and, 38
  importance of imagination in,
  37
  opposition to order of
  Neoclassicism, 81
*Romantic Triumph: American
Literature from 1830–1860,
The* (McDowell), 39
Rosenthal, Bernard, 84
Rush, Benjamin, 80

Santayana, George, 69
Scarlet Letter, The (Hawthorne),
14, 17

allegorical paradox in, 144–45
form of, comparison with
  Moby-Dick, 36
function of allegory in, 146–47
Hawthorne on, 149
Schelling, Friedrich, 34
Schlegel, A.W., 35
sciences
  concept of nature influenced
    by, 48
  as corrupting influence, 133
  versus intuition/imagination,
    50
  nature as counterbalance to,
    90
  and rise of organicism, 35
  Thoreau on, 96
Scott, Sir Walter, 34
"Self-Reliance" (Emerson), 67
Shelley, Mary, 14
Shelley, Percy Bysshe, 14
Sherman, Stuart, 113
Simms, William Gilmore, 41
slavery
  American Romanticism's
    attack on, 23–24
  Whitman on, 116, 117
  see also abolitionist movement
Smith, Sydney, 24
Socialism, Whitman on, 118
Song of Myself (Whitman), 57, 87
"Song of the Rolling Earth"
  (Whitman), 156
"Spiritual Laws" (Emerson),
  130
Staebler, Warren, 52
Stevens, Wallace, 104
Stibitz, E. Earl, 47
Stowe, Harriet Beecher, 23
*Study of English Romanticism,
  A* (Frye), 87
Sumner, Charles (U.S. senator),
  31
symbolism
  in *Moby-Dick*, 149–54
    land and sea, 150–51
    the white whale, 153
  problems in interpreting,
    151–52
  see also allegory

Taney, Roger B. (Supreme
  Court justice), 31
Tanner, Tony, 97
Taylor, Thomas, 63
Taylor, Zachary, 28
Thoreau, Henry David, 19, 32,
  38, 60, 75
  advocation of spirituality by,
    64
  and common man, 40
  as conservationist, 95–96
  as critic of industrialization,
    18
  on duty of the individual,
    109–10
  on expansion of
    communication, 30
  on the frontier, 41
  on government, 108, 110,
    111–12
  humanism of, 46–47
  on joy as condition of life, 70
  on money, 111
  role in antislavery movement,
    23–24
  and self-realization, 49, 50
  social criticism of, 56
  understanding of nature,
    93–95
Tolstoy, Leo, 114
"Tragic, The" (Emerson), 70
Transcendentalism, 60
  belief in self-knowledge, 21
  Coleridge's influence on, 34
  Emerson on, 19
  Hawthorne's rejection of, 23
  and individualism, 43
  influence on American
    Romanticism, 18–19
  optimistic nature of, 68–74
  origins of, 61, 65
  as outgrowth of Unitarianism,
    20
  rejection of materialism by, 22
  role of nature in, 75–77
  tenets of
    call for humility, 67
    the eternal ONE, 63–64
    intuitive thought, 66–67

progress as law of humanity, 71–74
simplicity, 64–65
trust thyself, 67
the world in God, 62–63
view of man, 112
"Transcendentalist, The" (Emerson), 62–63, 72–73
Traubel, Horace, 114, 117
Trilling, Diana, 126
Trollope, Anthony, 14
True Inspiration Society, 28
Turner, Frederick Jackson, 79, 83
Twain, Mark, 34, 120
Typee (Melville), 54, 120, 125, 151
Uncle Tom's Cabin (Stowe), 23, 30
Unitarianism
  influence on
  Transcendentalism, 20, 65
  as outgrowth of Calvinism, 33
Utopian communities, 28
Utopianism, 22
  and rise of American nationalism, 42
VanSpanckeren, Kathryn, 17
Very, Jones, 60
Walden (Thoreau), 56, 66, 87, 90, 98, 107
Walking (Thoreau), 87, 88
War of 1812, 27
Warren, Austin, 151
Warren, Robert Penn, 20
on Andrew Jackson, 16
on critical character of American literature, 58
Wayburn, Peggy, 85
Webster, Daniel, 30, 41
"When Lilacs Last in the Dooryard Bloom'd" (Whitman)

Whipple, E.P., 143, 144
White Jacket (Melville), 121
Whitman, Walt
  editorials of, 116
  as first city poet, 29
  humanistic view of, 47
  individualistic radicalism of, 115
  invention of free verse by, 15
  on language, 155
  patriotism of, 17
  and self-realization, 49, 50
  on slavery, 116, 117
  social criticism of, 56–57
  on socialism, 118
Whittier, John Greenleaf, 23, 32
  as abolitionist writer, 30
  and common man, 40
Wilbur, Richard, 133
wilderness
  American desire to tame, 80
  primary views of, 79
Wilson, William, 156
"Winter Walk, A" (Thoreau), 90
With Walt Whitman in Camden (Traubel), 114
Women in the Nineteenth Century (Fuller), 19
women's suffrage movement, 31
Woodlief, Ann, 92
Wordsworth, William, 14, 37, 57
  on nature, 99
Yeats, William Butler, 69
"Young Goodman Brown" (Hawthorne), allegory in, 145–46
Ziff, Larzer, 13